Culture and the Human Body

Culture and the Human Body

An Anthropological Perspective

John W. Burton

Connecticut College

WAVELAND

PRESS, INC.

Prospect Heights, Illinois

For information about this book, write or call:
Waveland Press, Inc.
P.O. Box 400
Prospect Heights, Illinois 60070
(847) 634-0081
www.waveland.com

Cover   Woman with piercings and tattoos. (www.TFPhoto.com)

Frontispiece   A worshipper pokes giant pins through his cheeks on Phuket Island, 428 miles southwest of Bangkok, during the 1997 Phuket Vegetarian Festival, a Chinese Buddhist celebration held annually to dispel bad luck. (AP/Wide World Photos)

Contents

    and the Body   51
    The Myth of Race   52
    The Ethnicity of Names   54
    Body Sense   56
    Body Images   57
    The Face of Culture   60
    Manufactured Bodies   61
    Identity on the Skin   63
    Temporary Skin   66

4   Him and Her: Initiation and the Body   69
    Ritual and Status   70
    The Sambian World   73
    Women and Men in Wogeo   77
    Kaguru Initiation and Morality   79
    Tiv Bodies   82
    Looking Back   85

5   Now and Then: Technology and the Body   89
    Human Population   90
    Culture and Reproduction   91
    Fashions of Conception   94
    Organs for Harvest and Sale   96
    Who Gets The Goods? An Applied Dilemma   97
    Technology, Life, and Death   99
    Euthanasia   102
    The Birth of Bioethics   103
    The Culture of Narcissism   105
    Some Closing Thoughts   106

    Bibliography   109

    Index   121

I dedicate these thoughts and this commentary to
my parents, Milton Campbell Burton and
June Katherine Burton, in thanks for their
persistent support in this sometimes difficult thing
we call life. They gave me mine and have supported
me in the way I have chosen to live it.
Children can ask no more from their parents.

Acknowledgments

One of the unique benefits of working, teaching, and learning in the environment of a liberal arts college is that one is perpetually offered the opportunity and challenge to grow beyond the boundaries of narrowly defined academic specializations. The graduate research university that thrives in North America evolved from a German model wherein the highest goal was precise and narrow academic specialization. Conversely, the liberal arts tradition had a classical origin, where knowledge of the world in its broad interdependence was the goal—an effort to see the interrelatedness of phenomena, rather than their seemingly singular character. For a bit more than twenty years I have worked in this environment, and have come to appreciate fully that academic disciplines or "departments" serve administrative needs but don't *really* correspond to, or represent, what faculty actually do. All academic work is interdisciplinary, as is all academic teaching and learning. As an anthropologist, working within a discipline that spans the gamut of human space and time, I have come to believe that the field is ideally situated in a liberal arts curriculum. The late R. Francis Johnson, dean emeritus of the faculty at Connecticut College, shared a similar view, and I thank him again, now after his passing, for his moral and intellectual support in finding an intellectual home for my own view of the world. For those who serve on the Connecticut College staff I am particularly grateful to Gina Foster, Tina Falck and Steve Bustamonte, who have each supported this work in their particular ways.

Numerous students I have come to know have had an important influence on my thinking, and some have had a more particular impact in the writing of this book. I want especially to thank Jessica Ogden, Bethany Waywell, Rachael Brown, Matt Stromberg, Katie Zorena, Megan Deitchler, Sara Ono and Christina-Mai Takahashi.

Through a number of serendipitous events, Professor John Middleton taught my course on anthropological history and theory while I was on sabbatical leave completing this manuscript, and he used my office when he was on campus. Through no expressed intent of either of us, I began leaving passages of the text on my desk and found that when I returned to my office, he had read and edited them. The process became an established ritual in short time; given his extensive anthropological knowledge and considerable editorial experience, my thoughts have certainly benefited from his sage insights. Thanks are also due to Thomas Curtin of the Waveland Press for his encouragement, patience and editorial skills, and to Jeni Ogilvie, also at Waveland Press, for her professional skills and insights. Anyone who reads the book and is familiar with the music of James Taylor will note that chapter titles have been inspired by his song called "Valentine's Day."

To my wife, L'Ana, our daughter, Jona, and our son, Jason, go my lasting thanks for providing a center to my life.

Introduction
An Anthropology of the Human Body

Like every other animate species, our physical form is the primary distinguishing feature of our being. And, like other animals, our bodies are the vessel of our life. However, in the course of human evolution, cultural adaptations that our ancestors invented began to alter our physical form as well as our physiology. Thus, *unlike* any other animals, humans use their bodies according to cultural as well as natural laws. In many significant ways the human body, through culture, has transcended "nature." Arctic creatures have evolved thick layers of flesh, fur, and blubber to retain heat and maintain homeostasis. African elephants have fairly enormous ears, which serve as natural air conditioners to cool the blood in their massive bodies. In the course of cultural evolution, the invention of various technologies began to free the human species from environment-specific forms of adaptation. Across thousands of generations, our hominid ancestors developed cultural patterns of survival that eventually affected the ways in which our species confronted the powerful forces of natural selection.

We are of the stature we are, of the general weight we are, and of the intelligence we are in consequence of cultural rather than natural processes. We are omnivores and can subsist on an extraordinary range of resources, and we live pretty much where we decide to: indeed, we are able to create artificial environments for habitation. As far as we can be certain, this makes us unique as animate life forms. The human body is at one and the same time an obvious and yet mysterious consequence of cultural evolution.

It is in the nature of culture that the human body is also a powerful medium of symbolic expression. The human body is a cultural cos-

1

tume: it is decorated from birth to death by diverse cultural traditions
and is therefore at all times a medium of cultural communication.

We likewise live our cultured lives through our bodies: what we
regard as food, who eats together, where we sleep and who sleeps
together, where and how we live, how we die and what happens to the
body following death are all *directly affected by culture*. It is in the
nature of culture that none of us—whether we are from Ontario or Oki-
nawa—decided what our first language would be, who our parents
would be, or how we would be socialized to accept *a particular* way of
being human as *the* way of being human. From the perspective of modern anthropology it is critically important to understand that the variety of cultural forms that exist in the present world, like those in the
past, are essentially arbitrary and contrived. There is no such thing as
"natural culture"—or for that matter, human nature (Geertz, 1973).
The distinguished Oxford anthropologist Rodney Needham (1978: 2)
has made this point more gracefully than I am able:

> We cannot just accept life. To the extent that we might do so we should
> not be living; we would be surviving, subsisting, just continuing. Rest-
> lessly, instead, we seek further satisfactions, not only because we are
> avid creatures but also because we live our lives within one form or an-
> other of civilization, and it is a gage of civilization that it creates de-
> sires and provides means to satisfy them. None of these desires is
> entirely natural, few are simple, and most are highly contrived.

In fact, the human body has been put to use by societies across time
in sometimes bewildering and certainly diverse ways. For the Romans,
public homicide was a matter of deep cultural and political significance:
gladiators murdered each other not only in self-defense but also as a
means of promoting the status of those in political power (Plass, 1995). In
ancient Greece, tattoos were inscribed on the body as a means to publicize
occupation and social status. For example, people who were condemned to
work in mines *(metalla)* were tattooed on their foreheads; slaves were likewise marked on the skin as a permanent declaration of their inferior social
status (Gustafson, 1997). During World War II the Japanese government
enslaved thousands of Korean women to serve as full-time prostitutes for
its armies (Hicks, 1994). Countless battles have been waged between
enemy peoples wherein the savage destruction of millions of people was
predictable and condoned. Conversely, there are examples of "honorable
suicide" in human history. More recently, we have instituted the altruistic
donation of body organs, sometimes during life and sometimes just after
death. The sale of sexual behavior is explicitly prohibited in most of North
America, even while male and female prostitution is commonplace (see,
e.g., Bell, 1994; Bristow, 1983; Carmen and Moody, 1985; Millet, 1971;
Weisberg, 1985; West, 1993). The social uses of the human body are as
diverse as the fundamental presumptions of different human cultures.

   This brief monograph attempts to offer a broadly historical and comparative study of various ways in which the human body is controlled, defined, celebrated, and transformed by human culture—in prehistory and at the present. My essential argument is that "the body" is a primary focal point of cultural expression and meaning. Just as there is no such thing as a pure gift, there is no such thing as a "natural" body. In recent years a fair amount of literature has been published on this topic; it falls into two broad categories. There are works such as Karl Groning's (1998) *Body Decoration* that feature glossy photographs and emphasize the oddity of otherness. In the other camp, which includes a raft of books on "modern primitivism," are numerous essays and monographs written in the dense jargon of postmodernism. (In one of my recent courses I assigned one such essay [Lock 1993]. When I arrived in class, students seemed unusually quiet, even a bit edgy. Eventually a student asked timidly, "Professor Burton, are you *angry* with us?" "Of course not," I answered. "Why would you think that?" She replied, "*Then why did you make us read that article?*" It was the sort of essay you read three times and still don't know what it was about). This book, unlike those cited, is not wedded to any particular theoretical paradigm. Indeed as the anthropologist T. O. Beidelman (1997: x) has suggested, social phenomena require multiple models and modes of interpretation:

> No single theoretical system entirely explains any society. A resourceful anthropologist employs different, even seemingly contradictory, analytical means to comprehend any manifold society and culture. Different theoretical approaches are useful in order to grasp different topics and problems.

When considering a topic as diverse as culture and the human body this advice is well taken.

   Anthropology is a vast discipline with ever-increasing specializations. Contemporary anthropologists study topics as diverse as the distribution of diseases in prehistoric human populations to the social organization of cyberspace communities. An "anthropology of the body" does not fit neatly into any preexisting focus of anthropological inquiry, but instead spans the boundaries of many fields of inquiry. This in turn indicates that "the body" is likewise a multifaceted concept and phenomenon: our bodies are the perpetual medium of all that transpires in our existence, from birth until death. A focus on the body is thereby an ideal means to investigate the diverse ways in which human cultures give meaning and form to life itself.

   Some of the ideas in this book grew out of two seminars I recently taught called "The Anthropology of Body Image." The first chapter asks the reader to speculate, on the basis of widely accepted scientific findings, about the role of culture in the process of human evolution. The field of paleoanthropology is founded upon sparse and sometime conflicting data, even while most contributors to this investigation agree that human evolution significantly altered the otherwise predictable laws of natural selection. We proto-humans made ourselves. Our instinct for language use (and thus for invention) resulted in a species that physically transformed itself. There is no record of a similar process in the archives of mammalian or primate evolution.

One of the most significant consequences of this evolutionary history is that we developed an instinct and a need to live in social groups. We don't always achieve this successfully, but it is in our evolutionary inheritance to make the effort. The human instinct for language is the strongest evidence of this fact. Social behavior, like language use, is predicated on the existence of rule-governed norms. A further discussion of these matters forms the basis of chapter 2. The basis of social and cultural identity provides the core of chapter 3. For all humans, a sense of self-reference and self-identity is the consequence of the tendency to distinguish "us" from "them." The human body is a primary tool in the process. Chapter 4 offers a number of perspectives on the ways in which different human cultures define and distinguish sexuality and gender. Here the concern is not with sexuality per se. Defining human sexuality (apart from its role in reproduction) is as improbable as defining eroticism. Rather, a number of ethnographic cases are reviewed in order to emphasize the arbitrary ways in which "natural" sexuality is given form and meaning by various cultural traditions. In the last chapter I raise a number of questions in relation to contemporary North American culture. Modern medical technology is stretching the limits of what we once thought we were and is likewise challenging moral and legal axioms about what we might become. State, provincial, and federal governments have an ever-growing control over the definition of human life.

As advances in medical technology emerge, humanity at large faces novel ethical dilemmas. During a class presentation on the topic of technology and the human body, Bethany Waywell noted the following information:

- The Herman J. Muller Repository for Germinal Choice, founded by Robert K. Graham in the late 1970s, collects sperm from Nobel Prize winners and Olympic athletes and offers insemination to women under 35 with high intelligence quotients.

- A recent survey of married couples in New England found that 1 percent would abort a fetus on the basis of sex, 6 percent if the child was likely to develop Alzheimer's disease, and 11 percent if the child was deemed predisposed to obesity.

- A 1988 survey conducted in Bombay, India, found that 7,999 out of 8,000 abortions had been based on knowledge through amniocentesis about the sex of the fetus. Each of those aborted was female.

- Nearly 90 percent of employees who work with computers for more than three hours a day suffer from some kind of eye inflammation.

- Over 33.9 million automobile accidents occur each year in North America, resulting in the deaths of 47,000 people and various injuries for 5.4 million others.

- Biotechnology industries and the United States Food and Drug Administration have decided that biotech crops do not require labels warning users of possible side effects from radiation and genetic manipulation of products.

- More than 400 different pesticides are used in growing the food we eat. No system is in place to reduce public exposure to these toxic chemicals.

- Seventy to 90 percent of all cancers are caused by industrial production and are thus theoretically preventable.

- Human organs have become commodities in many countries. For example, officials of the Chinese government transplant organs from prisoners approximately 2,000 times a year; India has an open, legal market for organ transplants; in Brazil, the state owns the body after death; in South Africa, officials can remove human organs from corpses without the consent of next of kin as long as a "reasonable attempt" at notification is made.

- As of 1997, an estimated 62,994 people in North America were registered on waiting lists for organ transplants.

- In the United States beginning in the early 1900s, local statutes condoned eugenic sterilization for those considered to be feeble-minded or genetically defective. Between 1907 and 1964, 64,000 people were sterilized under these laws.

- Since 1981, more than 70,000 babies in North America have been born through assisted reproductive technologies, more than half via in vitro fertilization.

These data clearly point to an emerging trend in regard to technology, culture, and the human body. They likewise present fundamental challenges to received moral and ethical norms. Technological innovation, however, is hardly a novel development across the span of human evolution; nor, for that matter, is it a novel circumstance that material and cultural changes create ethical dilemmas. There can be no conclusion to this chapter since technological innovations appear to emerge at an ever-increasing pace, proving yet further evidence of the ways in which human culture and imagination transforms the human body.

Chapter One

Human Evolution and Human Culture

PROLOGUE: WHERE WE ARE

In premodern times members of all human societies typically imagined that who they were and where they were was the measure of all things. The Nuer of the southern Sudan would tell an anthropologist in the 1930s that the tree from which the first human beings emerged was still standing along the bank of the Nile River. Until the period of first contact with Europeans in the 1930s, peoples living in the highlands of New Guinea were certain they were the only human beings in the world. Medieval philosophers, theologians, and cartographers were certain that one or another city marked the center of the universe, the point where humanity was conjoined with divinity. Well into the fourteenth century many Europeans assumed that the earth was flat. The belief—and in the case of Galileo, the discovery—that the earth circled the sun was considered heresy. More recently, Charles Darwin was ridiculed for suggesting that simple forms of life emerged into more complex forms and that human beings evolved from simian ancestors.

Perhaps a singular theme underlies these musings: our thoughts, our minds, and our bodies are constituted by the cultures into which we are born. Our sense of who we are is relative to our sense of where we are. As far as we can be certain, we are unique as a species in possessing a sense of self-consciousness and agency: this is me, this is what I can do. Although numerous animal species have complex means of communication, humans are unique in their use of language: it is a species-specific trait that evolved simultaneously with the emergence of our physical form and culture itself. Indeed, it is our capacity—or even

stronger, our instinct—to use language that gives rise to our consciousness and self-assessment and our ability to manufacture culture.

Knowing we are mortal (and now having seen the blue and white
orb of earth from the blackness of space many times), we seem all the
more intent on finding or deciphering our place in the universe. Closer
to home, we also seek to understand our origins. The academic field
known as paleoanthropology has emerged to try to answer some of
these complex questions.

Paleoanthropology is a field of inquiry concerned with the prehistory of evolving humans and evolving human culture. In the past, specialists in the field interpreted these topics largely through the examination of fossil remains and elements of material culture. In recent
years paleoanthropology has made significant advances through
sophisticated studies of DNA and genetics. The record of human evolution no longer appears as a single track, with one evolving into the next.
It is more useful to think of the process as a series of ponds, one spilling
into another, and then the next.

The human archaeological record and the fossil record of the past
50,000 years are dense, but they dissipate rapidly the further back we
look across time. In fact, the vast majority of this record will never be
recovered. Although the history of human evolution is a fascinating
story (some of this will be summarized in what follows), it is prudent to
keep it in perspective. Contemporary astronomers estimate that the
universe is from 13 to 15 billion years old. Imagine our sun as a
medium-sized orange, placed in the middle of Boston. The next sun
nearest our own is a similar-sized orange, sitting in Miami some 1,500
miles away. If you then imagine walking slowly from Boston to Miami,
you would be traveling hundreds of thousands of miles faster than any
spacecraft we could presently conceive of. The lesson is simple: our 3
million–year process of evolution is hard to comprehend, but it is only
a heartbeat on the scale of interstellar space.

That we can know such things is clearly the result of intelligence
rather than instinct. But it must be stressed that knowledge and intelligence are the product of culture and a particular way of thinking.

Sir Edward Tylor, one of the first academic anthropologists, defined
culture in a terse but powerful way. In essence, culture is everything that
human beings learn. This constitutes just about everything we do and
think. The proto-human invention of culture is the singular cause of our
evolutionary success, and it was the invention of culture that began to
transform the human body throughout our evolutionary history, continuing at present. At some point in this saga, individuals imagined,
"That's a rock, but it can be made into a tool." Culture and intelligence
are transforming. Instinct is homeostatic. The emergence of culture not
only transformed the way we once lived, but likewise transformed the
human body in the process. Indeed, the fossil record of human evolution

is the record of the changing human and prehuman body, which was transformed by increasingly complex prehistoric culture.

The precise details will ever elude us, but the eminent paleoanthropologist Richard Leakey (1994: xv) provides the big picture of human evolutionary history in four stages:

> The first was the origin of the human family itself, some seven million years ago. . . . The second was the proliferation of bipedal species. . . . Among this proliferation of human species was one that, between 3 million and 2 million years ago, developed a significantly larger brain. The expansion in brain size marks the third stage that led through Homo erectus and ultimately to Homo sapiens. The fourth stage was the evolution of modern humans—the evolution of people like ourselves, fully equipped with consciousness, artistic imagination, and technological innovation unseen elsewhere in nature.

The central argument of this first chapter is intended to "flesh out" Kingdon's observation (1993: 3): "the human form, human diversity, language and our relationship with nature have all been shaped by technology." He continues, "Humans have become increasingly different from apes by becoming artifacts of their own artifacts" (3). A sense of this process will emerge from what follows: (1) an overview of the fossil record of human evolution and some of the consequences of bipedalism; (2) the ways in which the domestication of fire altered human culture and behavior; (3) some of the likely origins of human language and its consequences; (4) the more recent effects of plant and animal domestication.

SOME EVOLUTIONARY BASICS

Here I draw on Boyd and Silk's (1997) lucid book *How Humans Evolved*. According to evolutionary theory, individuals struggle to survive. Within and between species there is variation in general fitness, and as a result there is differential ability to adapt to changes in the local environment. Adaptability is inherited across generations. While the ability of any species to expand in number is always plausible, a local environment does not offer unlimited resources. Over the course of time adaptation results from competition among individuals within a particular species as well as from competition with other species. Highly complex adaptations, for example, the evolution of bipedalism from quadrupedal locomotion, are unlikely to arise in a single instance or over a short period of time. Instead, complex adaptations arise across time through the accumulation of smaller random changes by the process of natural selection.

OUR HOMINID RESUME

Throughout the twentieth century in sub-Saharan Africa pale-oanthropologists have unearthed numerous fossil remains of a hominid species called Australopithecus afarensis that lived approximately 4 million years before the present. The species was rather short in stature—a little more than four feet tall—and had a cranial capacity more chimplike than modern human (in the range of 400 cc as compared to 1,400 for modern humans). Specialists are convinced, however, that afarensis had made the definitive move from a mostly permanent arboreal existence to one that included the open savannah. The evidence for this interpretation comes from two sources: (1) changing dentition, and (2) a changing pelvic bone, somewhat intermediary between those of a chimp and a modern human.

For the nonspecialist it is sufficient to note that afarensis finds reveal a tendency toward more sharply pointed teeth, with relatively small grinding areas on the molars. Earlier proto-hominid teeth were stockier and well adapted to a vegetarian diet, where prolonged mastication is needed to make high-fiber food digestible. Likewise, the mandible or lower jawbone is intermediary between modern chimp and modern human forms. For the paleoanthropologist, significant changes in dentition are clear evidence of a change in diet, which in turn suggests a change in adaptation to the local environment.

The afarensis pelvic bone is of similar significance. Chimps are most often quadrupeds: though they will occasionally scamper short distances on two legs, the normal mode of locomotion is "knuckle-walking." The chimp pelvis is elongated, thereby distributing body weight when walking with both arms and legs. In contrast, the afarensis pelvis is flattened, flared and considerably shorter. Also, in contrast to chimps, afarensis femurs or legbones are thicker and denser. Further, the afarensis knee bone has shifted inward, providing a more efficient means to center body weight for upright, bipedal locomotion.

Remains such as some fossil teeth, jawbones, pelvic bones, and the occasional femur are typically the only materials to work from in configuring the hominid lineage. However, specialists are able to reconstruct species in incredible detail from such scant data. Afarensis surely was no "missing link," but based on these fossil remains paleoanthropologists are certain that the species was in fact an intermediary hominid ancestor.

The gradual emergence of bipedalism is significant in numerous ways. For example, bipedalism required two fewer limbs for locomotion. This simultaneously freed the arms and hands for other activities and behaviors. Emergent bipedalism also offered new environments for habitation as well as new dangers and challenges. A number of these developments appear in association with Homo habilis, or "handy man," a species that lived approximately 2 million years before the present. The species was so named because of the numerous stone tool assemblages found at habilis sites. The earliest *known* manufactured stone tools were indeed the work of habilis. The species had a cranial capacity of approximately 800 cc, fully double that of afarensis. The gross increase in cranial size, however, is of less significance than the reasons for this increase. Perhaps the most important point to stress is that habalis's cranial capacity was increasing because of the evolution of an increasingly complex brain. Functional specialization of the brain is of greater significance than cranial capacity per se. As the habilis cranium was growing in size, facial bones were changing, too, emerging into a more rounded face. With habilis, the evolution of a more human-like jaw continues apace.

The habilis record we possess indicates evidence of an ancestral hominid population with two defining features that continue with modern humans: a mode of adaptation that is dependent upon language and the need to live in fairly small, stable groups, both for subsistence and for the protection of group members. The manufacture of stone and perishable tools, a more complex brain, regular bipedalism and greater mobility all suggest that hunting game or scavenging kill sites and collecting edible plants were increasingly common habilis activities. Success in this effort could only have been efficient if undertaken collectively. If food was gathered collectively, it was most probably eaten collectively.

Some specialists argue that a form of verbal communication must have accompanied these activities and all they entail. With the advent of bipedalism, the physiology of the throat and larynx were also modified, allowing for greater variation in the production of sound. Language use would have had extraordinary adaptive and selective value, not only for collective hunting and foraging but also for the manufacture of material culture. A simple hypothetical scenario provides an example. We have habilis group A and habilis group B. Group A has a simple, if effective, language, and Group B has none. Which group is more likely to produce better tools 100,000 years later? Figure into this equation an increasingly complex brain growing during gestation, but growing significantly larger after birth. The habilis brain was growing larger because survival meant learning more—about the manufacture of material culture, about hunting and foraging as techniques for survival, and equally important, about how to reside together in relatively stable social groups. Each of these tasks was as complex as the other.

Homo erectus was a later human ancestor that made the full-time adaptation to bipedal locomotion, and thus became able to adapt to almost any environment that offered sources of food and materials for tools. Remains of the erectus tool kit show remarkable similarities, whether found in Africa, Europe, or Southeast Asia.

Erectus fossils and material culture indicate that by 1.8 million years before the present erectus individuals walked fully upright, with the head balanced nearly atop the center of gravity. Adults were about five and a half feet tall and supported by a robust skeleton. The erectus cranium had become thicker, the forehead was receding, the face was broad and fairly flat, and the jaw was smaller still than those of earlier members of the fossil genealogy. Significantly, the ratio of the size of the pelvic opening relative to the size of the infant's head was essentially the same as that in modern humans. For erectus, as for us, a great part of cranial growth occurred after birth. Indeed, one of the signature features of this species is a cranial capacity in the range of 1,000 cc, a modest but notable increase over habilis. By the time erectus disappears from the archaeological record about 300,000 years ago, cranial capacity had grown to 1,100 cc—approaching nearly the range of modern humans.

Related changes in the facial musculature inferred from other morphological data indicate that erectus teeth were well adapted for tearing, biting, and chewing, suggesting in turn that hunting and meat eating had become commonplace. The stone tool kit—called Acheulean—was the most sophisticated to date in the hominid record and also apparently the most efficient: it remained basically unchanged for nearly 1 million years.

The absence of innovation in regard to stone technology implies that erectus had attained a homeostatic adaptation to local resources. Life wasn't necessarily nasty, brutish, and short, but neither was it a period in human prehistory that called for radical innovation. However, the inventory of erectus manufactured goods points to a number of culminating events. Manual dexterity had become a sophisticated tool of adaptation. Manual dexterity in turn provides evidence of an increasingly complex brain capable of more abstract cognitive tasks—such as language and a division of human labor. As the species evolved, it became increasingly unable to care for itself in any "natural" way. In other words, by the time of erectus, human culture was coming to supercede natural selection in charting the future of the human body.

THE DOMESTICATION OF FIRE

As noted earlier, erectus remains are found widely in Africa, Europe, and Asia. Whereas the first erectus populations of Africa could supplement their diet with tropical fruits or berries, in the cooler environments of Europe and central Asia vegetal resources would have been scarcer and available only on a seasonal basis. Specialists suggest that as erectus colonized these supratropical lands, meat became an increasingly important part of the diet. We will never know when erectus first used fire, but in time it became a regular part of adaptive culture. Any number of scenarios is plausible, and the safe bet is that it was by accident rather than design. Perhaps a wandering group of individuals happened through a forest recently burnt by lightning and came upon animal corpses caught in the blaze. The scavenged flesh surely would have been easier to eat, and perhaps more tasty than its raw form.

In the most elemental sense, cooking food is a way of predigesting it. Cooking quickly breaks down complex compounds into more digestible forms and also releases nutritious juices and flavors. The regular use of fire in this way (in essence, regulating a natural phenomenon via a cultural technique) had physiological consequences for erectus. Cooked meat, when compared to raw or cooked vegetal foods, provided considerably greater energy and calories to the diet. If meat consumption was an increasingly common activity, it may well be that erectus groups migrated from Africa in the way they did following seasonal migrations of game, to supplement other foraged food.

A famous archaeology site is located in the near vicinity of Beijing, at Zhoukoudian, China. It is a cave that was occupied by multiple erectus generations beginning 500,000 years before the present. Here paleoanthropologists have found hundreds of erectus stone tools, large quantities of butchered animal remains, all embedded in layers of charcoal and ash. One ash bed measures 22 feet in depth—a telling index of long and continual habitation. The site is widely held to be the first *certain* evidence of "domesticated" or controlled fire use in human prehistory. This was also a home-base site: not a prehistoric city, but a prehistoric retreat, to which erectus individuals returned day after day, month after month, generation after generation.

Although this is the first certain evidence of regular fire use in prehistory, it is highly likely that fire was a part of the erectus tool kit long before. If this is the case, the real significance of the Zhoukoudian site is that it proves that erectus populations lived in social groups on a regular and long-term basis. Fires were probably set in strategic locations to drive game toward hidden hunters or into bogs and mire where the animals would be trapped. The odds that a hunting technique such as this might survive in the archaeological record are infinitely improbable, but the likelihood of using fire in this way seems certain. In any case employing fire at all made erectus unique in the animal world. No other species controls and uses nature in this way.

The domestication of fire had manifold consequences for erectus material culture and also must have had an effect on the evolving moral and imaginative world of these hominid ancestors. We see vestiges of this in our own lives. Hundreds of thousands of North Americans spend hours by campfires on camping trips. Sharing food cooked outside over an open fire is likewise a common element of contemporary culture. In North America, an intimate evening in front of a blazing fire is a symbol of lustful pleasure. Fire was both a cultural artifact and a valuable means of promoting sociable behavior. The "fire in the cave" environment provided a nesting ground for emotional and cognitive attachment to others. The culture of fire also effected biologically regulated diurnal cycles among erectus groups. No longer regulated by the natural cycles of daylight and evening, domesticated fire prolonged daylight into the night, which no doubt assisted the further development of language and social skills.

Contemporary research also suggests that domesticated fire had other effects on the human body, particularly in regard to the distribution of body hair. By the time of erectus, the regular use of fire lessened the adaptive value of thickly distributed body hair as a means to regulate body temperature. Fire was a culminating factor in a process of thinning body hair that began earlier in our evolutionary history. Indeed, the gradual loss of body hair began in association with early bipedalism. Though not literally correct, Desmond Morris titled his popular book on human evolution *The Naked Ape*. Our early hominid ancestors were most likely a pileous lot, perhaps resembling Bonobo chimps in the distribution of body hair. In a humid tropical environment typical of where contemporary nonhuman primates live, a thick coat of body hair has adaptive value, since this creates a microenvironment for cooling skin temperature. Some time ago, Wheeler (1984) pointed out that as bipedalisam emerged, less body hair would have adaptive value.

Wheeler argues that bipedalism required a very efficient way of cooling the body. Every human has between 2 to 5 million sweat glands. From birth until puberty the greatest concentration of hair is on the head. This makes good sense to Wheeler. As a bipedal species our greatest exposure to sunlight is on the top of the head, unlike a quadruped, where the entire topside of the elongated body is exposed to the sun. Relative hairlessness had adaptive value since this promoted cooling of the body through sweat and evaporation. Residual head hair had adaptive value since this helped to protect the growing hominid skull (and thus brain) from extreme and thus threatening heat. In short, the increasingly mobile hominid shed body hair to promote efficient locomotion.

A complementary interpretation of hominid hair loss is offered by Sheets-Johnstone (1990). She notes that one of the most commonly observed behaviors of contemporary chimps is intensive dyadic grooming. Chimps will sit for long spells picking at one another's fur, cleansing each other of ticks, lice, and other vermin. Authorities interpret this as a behavior that promotes bonding and social solidarity. Sheets-Johnstone suggests that in the course of bipedal evolution group-based subsistence activities (foraging, hunting) replaced grooming as the primary means of achieving this in early hominid groups. She argues that intensive dyadic grooming was an impediment to subsistence activities. Fur and grooming, in other words, were not adaptive for free-ranging bipeds. As Sheets-Johnstone writes:

> Furry individuals elicit more grooming and need more grooming than non-furry ones. They are unable to devote as much time to communal subsistence. Moreover, fur is a direct impediment to direct body touching and thus to the realization of maximum skin to skin contacts and tactile pleasure. Stroking is a distinctly human act, a distinctly gratifying one. . . . Loss of fur was thus an adaptation both to a newly developing social structure and to a newly developing sexuality. Expressed in classic adaptationist terms, selection favored those creatures with less fur both because of the decreasing social value of fur and because of its increasingly negative sexual value. (1990: 39)

Thus, the advent of controlled fire added a cultural innovation that amplified a biologically adaptive trend in hominid evolution. With fire in the cultural background, a relatively hairless body would not only render it more responsive to stimulation, but it would also be a less likely host to fleas, lice, or ticks. Domesticated fire not only changed our diet but also served to transform the body. As suggested, the regular use of fire promoted more complex social and cognitive skills.

THE DOMESTICATION OF MIND

Which factors would have encouraged the emergence of what Pinker (1994; see also Cheney and Seyfarth, 1990; Chomsky, 1988; Cummins and Allen, 1992; Gibson and Ingold, 1986; Humphrey, 1993; Laitman, 1984; Wills, 1993) has termed the human language *instinct?* There are many, and they are varied, and the question has spawned generations of learned debate.

The origin of human language is one of the most perplexing issues in hominid evolution. There is a great deal that we don't know, so it is best to begin by listing a number of features about human language about which there is absolute certainty.

First, language is governed by rules, and some of these appear to be common to all natural human languages. The human brain is therefore "hard-wired" for language use. We know this in part from the detailed study of numerous functional specializations of the brain. Specific areas of the brain have specific linguistic functions. Second, human languages are perpetually in the process of change, particularly in regard to the lexicon, or meaningful words in a language. Third, language usage is a fundamental prerequisite for the existence and continuity of social groups. Fourth, human beings learn language instinctively, sometimes as many as three or four at the same time. Fifth, we will never know precisely how or when human language evolved. "Primitive" language left no fossil record. Some further prefatory remarks are necessary, particularly regarding some important differences between natural human languages and animal communication systems.

Simply defined, a human language is a system of pairing sound with meaning. Human physiology allows for more control and manipulation of sound than any other animal species. Unlike animal communication systems, human language is a voluntary behavior. Animal communication systems are closed and invariant while human languages can produce a theoretically infinite number of meanings based on a limited number of sounds. Human language is obviously the basis of abstract and analytical thought. We think not just about the here and now but also about how Dante may have felt when *The Inferno* was completed and about what the first flight of humans to Mars will entail. While language allows us to "displace" thought or information in this way, the spoken word is extinct the moment it is uttered. Many animals communicate by scents that can linger for days—on the sides of fire hydrants, for example. Unlike animal communication systems, we can consciously make changes in human languages, or alter what we just said.

The complex phenomenon of language has not evolved among other animal species because there has been no selective advantage for this to occur. Animal brains are largely homeostatic, regulating the here and now. A dog can no more stop itself from barking when threatened than a bee can stop itself from "dancing." These are involuntary behaviors. African vervet monkeys have three distinct alarm calls, which are used in three distinct situations of threat—no more, no less. And whenever a predatory hawk appears, out goes the call. Although we may experience an involuntary physiological reaction in a threatening circumstance, our language and intelligence allow us to do an extraordinary number of different things—or even nothing at all. We don't instinctively shriek upon sighting a leopard: we can sit still and say nothing at all. We can say, "Jeez, that is a REALLY BIG ROCK rolling toward me!" or something casual or ironic such as "Vuja de—yikes. I'd never want to be here again." It is best to regard animal communication systems as signal systems and human languages as symbol systems. It is the ability to communicate thought rather than thought itself that makes language so unique to our species.

In terms of physiology, internal complexity and specialization, no other mammal has a brain sophisticated enough to "do" language. As Noam Chomsky has argued, the intelligent part of the human brain is the language organ. Mind, he has said, is what the brain does. This has come at some cost in evolutionary terms. While the brain comprises only about 2 percent of body weight, it consumes 20 percent of the oxygen we inhale. The female pelvis has the form it does in part to allow for the birth of a baby with a large head. As every parent knows, an infant's head is awkwardly out of proportion with its tiny body.

LANGUAGE AND CULTURE

The evolution of the capacity (if not the need) for speech and abstract thought was rooted in the production and reproduction of human existence in prehistory. The manufacture of material culture, the regular use of fire, living and foraging in social groups: these are forms of *cultural* behavior, which therefore must be *learned*. The preponderance of stone tools manufactured by erectus were made for use with the right hand. Right handedness and language functions are largely controlled in the left side of the hemisphere. Language and manual dexterity evolved in tandem. With regard to early hominid tool use and language evolution Greenfield (1991) has examined this matrix of form following function in careful detail.

Although highly technical in exposition, her thesis is elegantly simple: manual dexterity became more sophisticated as a consequence of increasing linguistic capability. The "modular" manufacture of material culture—first find the right stone, then hold it correctly, then turn it to the other side—is likened to the modular development of language and grammar. Greenfield suggests that within the human brain there is a common neural connection for language and object combinations. Language evolved, by this reasoning, in step with the hominid manipulation of the physical environment. The manufacture of material culture and language work on the basis of modular hierarchies. Simple tools have simple "grammars," as do simple utterances. Single utterances (Mama) are the basis for more complex notions (Mama come), which then become more highly refined (Mama come now!). This is in fact a model of the process by which all infants learn the language spoken around them.

Greenfield's thesis is not unlike that of Bickerton, a specialist in the study of pidgin and creole languages. In his important book *Language and Species* (1990) Bickerton argues that early hominid speech was probably akin to a newly forming pidgin language. Collectively, pidgin languages have a simple grammar and lexicon and have emerged throughout human history whenever there is sustained contact between peoples of different cultural and linguistic traditions. Given time and common interests, pidgin languages evolve into grammatically more complex creole languages. Bickerton suggests that early hominids, possibly of the erectus sort, spoke a proto-language resembling pidgin. By the logic of natural selection, selective advantage would favor linguistic usages that became more complex, and thus at the same time brains that could master these tasks.

It is hard to fault the logic of either of these models (and I have simplified their interpretations significantly); yet many authors in this field assert that "true" language usage was the crowning achievement of our more recent ancestors. The evidence of large kill sites, nearly permanent places of habitation, a diverse stone tool kit, and the use of fire—all associated with erectus remains—together would suggest that the regular use of language is as old as the regular use of bipedal locomotion. Pinker (1994: 369) suggests, "I suspect that evolving humans lived in a world in which language was woven into the intrigues of politics, economics, technology, family, sex, and friendship, that played key roles in individual reproductive success. They could no more live with a Me-Tarzan-You-Jane level of grammar than we could."

In that light an ethnographic analogy is useful. The phrase *ethnographic analogy* is used by archaeologists to flesh out an archaeological site that seems to resemble that of a living human society. I stress that the phrase is used as a heuristic device: *there is no human society that is a living relic of the "Stone Age."* The phrase simply asks, if we look at a contemporary society, can it help us to understand one from long ago? I draw here from a book by Liebenberg that examines in detail the hunting techniques of a group of !Kung foragers from southern Africa. He writes:

> While tracking down a solitary wildebeest spoor of the previous evening, !Xo trackers pointed out evidence of trampling which indicated that the animal had slept at that spot. They explained consequently that the spoor leaving the sleeping place had been made early in the morning and was therefore relatively fresh. The spoor then followed a straight course, indicating that the animal was on its way to a specific destination. After a while, one tracker started to investigate several sets of footprints in a particular area. He pointed out that these footprints all belonged to the same animal, but were made during previous days. He explained that the particular area was the feeding area of that particular wildebeest. Since it was, by that time, about midday, it could be expected that the wildebeest may be resting in the near vicinity. (1990: 146)

I repeat: the !Kung are modern humans like the rest of us. Given that fact, tracking a wildebeest 500,000 or a million years ago was no less complicated and demanding that it was ten years ago. The lesson from Pinker's (1994) assertion is self-evident: *the more complex early hominid language was, the more likely it was to have adaptive value.* In Sheets-Johnstone's (1990: 96–97) view, language use and upright posture didn't just free the hominid's hands, but freed the whole mind and body. This created a wholly different domain of "'I cans' and with it a host of radically different meanings." The emergence of linguistic competence in ancestral hominids was the *preeminent* tool in the handbag of hominid culture. As Pinker (1994) would have it, language was a biological adaptation for the communication of cultural knowledge. In this light, if one wants to speak about the evolution of human culture, one is at the same time involved in a dialogue about the evolution of human language, and the nature of human learning.

With the emergence of modern Homo sapiens, beginning about 300,000 years ago, culture had effectively adapted to nature. Growing cranial capacity was a biological process, but it was the consequence of cultural evolution. By this time, what had changed most in the record of human evolution was not so much the way we gained a livelihood, but the increasing refinement and efficiency by which it was done. Comparing the tool assemblages of erectus with Homo sapiens is akin to comparing the handwriting of a six-year-old with that of an adult. Following the cognitive revolution in human prehistory was a radical innovation that took place in an evolutionary heartbeat: the domestication of plants and animals, some 10,000 to 7,000 years before the present. This cultural innovation also had dramatic effects on the human body.

DOMESTICATED NATURE

Most archaeologists agree we may never know exactly when or how modern humans began to produce rather than forage food. There were certainly climatic and environmental factors at work. Once domesticated foods became the mainstay of human existence, however, the human body and the structure of social life were dramatically affected. This section provides a brief overview of perspectives on the process of domestication. A century ago technological innovations such as domestication, monumental architecture, and large cities were lauded as testimony to the "progress" of civilization. Domestication has had its down side as well.

The late British archaeologist V. Gordon Childe (1936; see also Farb and Armelegos, 1980; Leonard, 1973; Tannahill, 1988) is typically credited as one of the first modern thinkers to propose a theory to account for the origins of plant domestication. He argued that as glaciers from the last ice age retreated, deserts began to replace previously fertile grasslands and forest zones. He believed that agriculture began in the Nile valley in northern Africa, where peoples who once foraged for their livelihood were forced to settle along the banks of the Nile. To his mind, plant domestication was a bold and desperate stand for survival. Later, Robert Braidwood (see Leonard, 1973) argued that since the advanced civilization of Egypt was firmly established 5,000 years ago, domestication probably first took place elsewhere. He undertook field research in the Zagros Mountains of Iraq. Here, he said, there occurs in nature a remarkable constellation of the "natural" plant and animal species that eventually became the first domesticates of this region: wild wheat, barley, sheep, goats, pigs, cattle, and horses.

One of the sites Braidwood excavated is known as Jarmo, in northern Iraq. At the lowest level of the site (and hence the earliest period of human occupation, some 7,000 years ago) he found mortars and pestles used for grinding wheat and barley as well as sickle blades used for harvesting. The site also included bone fragments from sheep and goats, from which he inferred early attempts at domestication. Among other things, Braidwood's findings proved that Egyptian civilization emerged long after plants and animals had been domesticated in Southwest Asia. Further research later conducted in the same area revealed a significant trend. Starting about 20,000 years ago, he says, the remains of human animal kill sites showed that the species regularly hunted were becoming smaller and smaller. In other words, human hunters had overhunted or depleted larger game. His conclusion was that smaller game was kept under human control to assure a supply of food. Plants had been domesticated earlier, he pointed out, in order to feed the animals now under human control.

Except in Australia, domesticated plants and animals became common throughout the world over the past 5,000 years. Southwest Asia produced wheat, barley, sheep, pigs, goats, and cattle; forms of millet, sorghum, and yams were domesticated in western Africa; rice, sugarcane, and taro were cultivated in China and Southeast Asia; beans, corn, and squash were common in Central America; and potatoes were grown in Andean South America.

In each case there eventually emerged novel forms of human society, based on permanent settlements with ever-increasing populations. Indeed, the city-states of Southwest Asia, Pharoanic empires, Chinese dynasties, and the civilization of the Aztecs and Incas would not have emerged in the absence of domesticated plants and animals. It was only human culture, in this case, the control of natural species, that made this possible. The state-level societies that emerged shared numerous features in common, including monumental architecture, systems of recording information permanently, extreme social stratification, standing armies, and divine kings. To date, no single theory has been accepted about how the great Egyptian pyramids were erected or how the Aztec Temple of the Sun was made. However, it is certain that slave and conscripted labor played a major role in each case.

Some people imagine that the emergence of domesticated plants and animals were decisive achievements in human prehistory. Larsen (1995) has suggested otherwise. He notes that "the shift from foraging to farming led to a reduction in health status and well-being, an increase in physiological stress, a decline in nutrition" (186). As carbohydrates became the mainstay in early agricultural communities, vitamin deficiencies, as revealed by declining dental health, became common. He continues (198):

> Reduced population mobility and increased aggregation provided conditions that promote the spread and maintenance of infectious parasitic diseases. . . . That is, closer, more crowded living conditions facilitate greater physical contact between members of a settlement, and permanent occupation can result in decreased sanitation and hygiene. More densely settled agricultural societies were more prone to infection than were earlier groups. (See also Clark and Brandt, 1984; Cohen, 1977 and 1989.)

In short, the popular view that domesticated plants and animals improved the human condition is fundamentally incorrect.

Domestication also gave rise to "crowd diseases" as human population densities grew. According to Diamond (1988: 196):

> If the rise of farming was a boon for our microbes, the rise of cities was a veritable bonanza. . . . Another bonanza was the development of world trade routes, which by Roman times effectively joined the populations of Europe, Asia and North Africa into one giant breeding ground for microbes. . . . When we domesticated social animals such as cows and pigs they were already afflicted by epidemic diseases just waiting to be transferred to us. . . . For example, the measles virus is most closely related to the virus causing rinderpest. Rinderpest doesn't affect humans. Measles, in turn, doesn't affect cattle. The close similarity of the measles and rinderpest viruses suggests that the rinderpest virus transferred from cattle to humans, then became the measles by changing its properties to adapt to us.

Thus, domestication simultaneously created the condition for enormous population growth along with environments to breed diseases to limit it! Diamond's insight is powerful: endemic diseases were the result of cultural innovation.

The spread of these diseases had tragic consequences for peoples of the New World. The "Eurasian crowd diseases," as Diamond (1988) terms them, evolved from diseases in domesticated Eurasian herd animals. In the New World there were few domesticated animals other than the turkey, the guinea pig, the dog, the Muscovy duck, and the llama. When humans first began to populate the New World some fifteen to twenty thousand years ago, they never developed immunities to herd-spawned diseases. Diamond (1988) suggests, therefore, that the European conquest of the New World was largely a consequence of the introduction of Eurasian-derived crowd diseases. One of the most dramatic arenas in which this tragedy unfolded was that which pitted Cortés and his 600-man army against the million or more Aztecs of central Mexico. Diamond argues that what gave Cortés his real advantage was smallpox, which reached Mexico in 1520 with the arrival of one infected slave

from Spanish Cuba. The resulting epidemic killed nearly half the
Aztecs. North of the border, native populations suffered even worse.

Another dramatic example of the way in which human cultural
innovation affected the human body has been described in Livingstone
(1958). Prior to the introduction of iron technology in sub-Saharan
Africa, indigenous peoples were commonly foragers or practiced horticulture with stone technology. By 500 B.C. in northern Nigeria the Nok
culture emerged, known in the archaeological record by the domestication of yams and the use of metal tools. Over time, as greater areas of
forest were cleared for cultivation, growing populations migrated
south, east, and west. Over the following seven to eight hundred years
this process led to the peopling of what is now called Bantu Africa. In
the wake of these migrations human populations left behind them ideal
environments for malarial-bearing mosquitoes to breed. Former gardens, cleared of trees, formed seasonal pools and ponds of water. As the
human population grew, so too did the population of malarial-bearing
mosquitoes. Humans became the most plentiful and available blood
meal for mosquitoes and also the most ready host for the malarial-
borne parasite. The biological mutation of the sickle cell in humans
proved to be a positively adaptive mutation to this parasite. Presently,
there is a nearby exact correspondence between the distribution of
malarial-bearing mosquitoes and sickle cell–bearing humans in Africa.
As Livingstone (1955: 555) concludes, "the spread of agriculture is
responsible for the spread of the selective advantage of the sickle cell
gene, and hence for the spread of the gene itself."

THE DOMESTICATED HUMAN

In this review of some aspects of human prehistory I have high-
lighted data that point to the way in which human culture has super-
ceded natural process in the course of evolution and the ways in which
cultural innovations have variously affected the human body. An alien
observer of our world might regard our species as just another animate
form. That much is true, but the human is also an animal of its own
(unintended) design. Standing on the side of logic rather than evidence,
the French anthropologist Claude Lévi-Strauss has suggested that the
first artifact of human culture was the invention—better still, the convention—of the incest taboo. Whatever form this takes in any particular human society, it is in essence always the same: the artificial regulation of an otherwise natural process, namely, reproduction. Through
this ritual regulation we have at one and the same time altered the
course of our genetic inheritance and created the basic building block
of human society. Hominid evolution has been a consequence of an

emerging synergy among culture, intelligence, and mind. In fact, precious little that we see in the world before our eyes partakes of "nature" in pure form. Rather, "nature" is itself a cultural construct. The physical landscape is carefully groomed. A "nature preserve" is simply a physical environment that has been set aside for cultural purposes. A cultural recipe has filtered the water we drink. Surely there is no such thing as "natural" food, since in all human societies food is artificially produced and has particular cultural meaning. Even the air we breathe is laden with the residue of industrial production. Culture has created and dominates the human form.

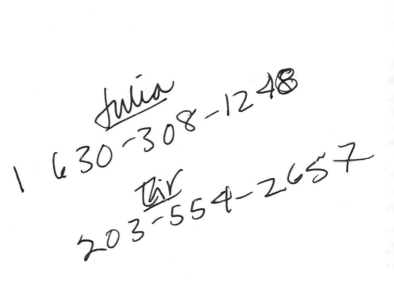

Chapter Two

You and Me
The Social Life of the Body

Cogito ergo sum: I think; therefore I am. This proposition has held the favor of numerous philosophers, but an anthropologist would be inclined to rephrase the matter this way: we are; therefore we think. Our minds and bodies are not self-willed, free-floating entities. The "self" is best regarded as a structure of beliefs, sentiments, and values and is therefore an extension and product of social existence. So too with the human body: our physical sense of self is decidedly a cultural construct. What we think about, how we sleep, how we walk and talk are all things that we learn to do. Even basic biological functions are mediated by learned cultural behavior. Of course we are individual, sapient beings, but only as a consequence of our biosocial nature.

This chapter provides an overview of some of the theoretical literature relating to the social construction of the body and self. As in chapter 1, it is not my goal to champion a particular paradigm. As the anthropologist Franz Boas argued a hundred years ago, any attempt to explain something as complex as culture by a single means is probably wrong. What we think we are, as well as *who* we think we are, is fundamentally the result of our interaction with others. Many of the leading contributors to modern social theory have put their own personal spin on this fundamental truth. A second aim of the chapter is to highlight the ways in which the human body serves as a representation of human culture. The chapter concludes by placing these generalizations in the context of particular ethnographic examples.

CULTURE AND THE BODY

The body mediates all that we do as intelligent, conscious beings. In a certain sense, this applies to all life forms. However, humans are body sensitive in distinct and unique ways. The human body is transformed in both conscious and unconscious ways. The conscious forms are what we think of as personal motivations: this is how I want to look today. The unconscious forms are what often confront us when we think, "What am I doing" and "Why?" A mundane example may illuminate this point. Almost everyone who drives has had the following experience. You have gone ten miles down the road at considerable speed, and then you suddenly realize: you are driving! But for the past ten minutes your mind has drifted across any number of memories or plans for the future. The *last* thing you have been thinking about is *driving*, even though you haven't had an accident. For some moments conscious attention drifts from the task at hand, namely, participating in highly rule-governed behavior. This is the nature of culture's impress on the unconscious. We most often do it on cruise control and take it for granted.

Unconscious cultural forms mediate not only conscious forms of experience—what we imagine, how we anticipate the future, what might be the best gift for a birthday—but also gut-level dimensions of life. What is food? Where is it found? How is it eaten? At the time of this writing 6 billion humans are working their way through these and far more complex decisions through some 5,000 different cultural "recipes." Conscious human motivations are largely the result of arbitrary cultural conventions, the time and place of our being.

The human body can be likened to a cultural mirror. The body is used to designate time and place. Clothing and body adornment serve to mark age, gender, personal, and ethnic affiliation. But this is not done in a species-specific manner or as a natural phenomenon, as it is when a certain species of snake molts its skin or a butterfly emerges from a chrysalis. Even "natural" body processes such as menstruation are mediated by distinct cultural practices. Indeed, there is nothing natural about body transformation: these are entirely governed by arbitrary cultural conventions. Every human culture presumes and imposes a particular body aesthetic across the life cycle: how it should be born and what it should look like in youth, middle age, and death. If this seems plain and obvious, it is only because we take our own customs to be the norm. There is nothing either plain or obvious about the ways in which culture manipulates the human body.

The fact is that while we regard our bodies as the fundamental basis of our intimate identity and sense of self, the body is a public medium and a public possession. In North America, unless a human birth is officially recognized with the proper piece of paper, the newborn has no legal or social status. Oddly, we are not officially dead until yet another document establishes the fact. Even when we sleep, we are not alone: often our dreams draw us into unexpected encounters with people, places, and circumstances.

The common theme underlying diverse and mundane customs such as how we are born, what we eat, where we eat, or how we adorn ourselves is that all these behaviors and expectations are governed by rules. Anthropologists have for some time asserted this interpretation: a culture is a system of rules. Although rules governing the body (and belief and behavior more generally) may seem arbitrary to the uninformed observer—Why do women wear masks over their faces? Why do those people burn their dead? —from the local perspective such practices are quotidian and rarely questioned. Indeed, to do something else would be odd.

As we know, some rules appear plain and simple—common sense as we call them. The common sense rules typically apply in the context of survival: don't stand in the middle of the railroad when a train is approaching at great speed; don't try to swim in freezing water; don't play with poisoned arrows, and so forth. Other rules make sense only within the matrix of a broader system of symbols, or a culture: representations that signify other relationships ordered on the basis of hierarchy and analogy. These latter rules comprise the vast majority of ways in which the body is controlled by culture. Don't eat meat on Friday. Don't eat during daylight during Ramadan. At a formal dinner, don't eat until the highest-status person has begun to eat. Survival rules? Hardly. These are culturally contrived rules of body control. Yet their symbolism is powerful. A further example may make the point clearer. Perhaps a driver once pulled you off the road with a blinking light on the top of his or her car. The individual then approached your car, clad in a carefully styled uniform, complete with a gun and tall boots, and demanded your license. Odds are you *didn't* say, "Hey, you're no cop—that's just a costume." Cops don't have to wear military "costumes" to be cops anymore than tennis players at Wimbledon have to wear white costumes to play tennis. But the costume provides us with a sense of who others are, what they do and what to expect as a result.

Beyond the basic body rules we unconsciously learn in infancy—how to stand, how to sit up, and eventually how to walk—the first rule-governed system we learn is language: rules about how to pair sounds with meaning. A language system, like a social or cultural system, is systematic precisely because it is an ordered grid of possibilities—a system of rules. In most cases two-year-olds are well down the road to mastering this task. However, typical two-year-olds are also exceptionally ego-centered (not egotistic!). Their surrounding world is atemporal and seems to be entirely focused on their individual selves. They may be sitting next to each other engaged in nearly identical "play" activities, yet virtually oblivious to each other's presence. By the age of three, the more serious task of interactive play begins.

Although no three-year-old is aware of the fact, play is serious work. Among other things, it is a process of continuing learning about encoding grammatical rules as well as cultural biases. A personal memory may help to make the point. When I was feeding my three-year-old son carrots, I encouraged him by saying, "Carrots are good for you! They will make your eyes strong." He responded, "Daddy, what is hamburger good for?" "Playing" (house, trucks, dolls, hide and seek) is really about learning fundamental skills of body control, social interaction, and the rules that govern each. "Play" is learning the acceptable bounds of behavior and the implicit rules and values of social life. Two contrasting examples further help to make this point.

Mbuti children (the so-called Pygmies of the Congo) learn when they play that they should give one of their favorite possessions to a playmate to have and to keep. Sharing and cooperative effort in the hunt is critical to Mbuti survival. Many North American parents can probably recall stories about occasions where young children break into rage and tears over *what is mine*, a value that is likewise central to consumer capitalism.

For the young child, learning the rules of language and social interaction is at the same time learning a process of learning the rules about the distinctive self in its mental and physical form: how to think in the company of some other and how to control the body. That they do this at the same time that they are very active language learners cannot be an evolutionary accident.

THE BODY FROM A DISTANCE

In current pedestrian discourse the word *theory* commonly refers to matters of little regard or consequence. Theory is contrasted to hard and real facts. In reality, however, facts do not have an independent existence outside a theoretical framework: things make sense only within the context of a broader cognitive scheme. Again, language serves as a useful model. Grammar is the underlying theory of any particular language. If we speak in a standard way, we can make sense and share ideas because we share an internalized and largely unconscious theory of language. Grammar sets the range and possibilities of language use. Likewise, theory explains and interprets fact. Theory is the forest when seen from afar—something you couldn't see standing in the midst of it.

Occasionally an anthropological account of the meaning of a particular behavior or belief is regarded with skepticism. Is an anthropologist's interpretation of an initiation ceremony, for example, consistent with what the participants might say it means? The same question can be asked in reverse: is the local account really more authentic? By definition, thinking analytically or abstractly entails "standing back" to gain a broader view.

This "insider/outsider" dichotomy is parallel to another dichotomy between that of conscious and unconscious experience. The French anthropologist Lévi-Strauss provided (at least to his satisfaction) an answer. In this view, the conscious explanation for a behavior (Why do you eat this? Because it tastes good.) is less an explanation and more a rationalization for a particular behavior. In other words, the local's account for the "why" of things is just as often a retort of "why not?" Anthropologists can provide many other examples: "It's what we have always done." "Our ancestors did it." "Nobody ever died from it." "Nobody knows anymore." Thus, in regard to cultural interpretation and meaning, the "native point of view" may be quite different from an anthropological interpretation. The Oxford anthropologist Godfrey Lienhardt (1964: 53) put the matter this way: "No social phenomenon can be adequately studied merely in the language and categories of thought in which the people among who it is found represent it to themselves." This view constitutes the very basis on which cross-cultural generalizations and interpretations are made. Theory is clearly central to interpretation.

THE COLLECTIVE AND THE INDIVIDUAL

General statements about the nature of social existence should pertain to all societies. By example, any general statement about human families, whether they are matrifocal, nuclear, extended, or single parent, should highlight features common to all forms. Since some form of "the family" is a human universal, this institution must attend to some common human issues. So, too, with the human body: what is the nature of the perpetual dialectic between the singular human body and the society that controls and molds it? In a general way, human societies create an image of the body in terms current at the time. For example, in North America since the Industrial Revolution, the body has been conceived of as a kind of machine. More recently human cognition has been likened to the working of a computer. Conversely, there are many metaphors that image society as a kind of body: the economy is "healthy"; newspaper reporters write about the "pulse" of local life; major "arteries" leading into cities become clogged, and so on.

One of the founders of modern social theory, Emile Durkheim, put forward a number of primary questions about the relationship between the social and individual worlds and stressed that "the individual" is largely the consequence of "the social." Arguing against the paradigm of Sigmund Freud, Durkheim insisted that individual behavior was best understood and therefore explained as a consequence of, rather than on the basis of, individual psychology or motivation. In this view, it is not individuals who create society. Rather, individuals are created within the context and constraints of society.

Many of Durkheim's major writings continue to be required reading in the realm of social theory. In his book *Suicide: A Study in Sociology* (1952 [1897]) Durkheim argues that this act, which might be thought of as a quintessential individual behavior, is in fact best understood as a social phenomenon. Durkheim observes a "seasonality" to suicide rates in European societies: they rise and fall in association with other social phenomena, in particular occasions of social significance, such as holidays and other secular and sacred observances. Those who feel most alienated from society are likely candidates for suicide on those occasions when group solidarity is collectively celebrated. (It is noteworthy to recall that suicide is illegal in most contemporary societies and is condemned as a sin in many world religions.) According to Durkheim, suicide occurs because people have not been sufficiently socialized or otherwise controlled by social values and norms. In societies where rates of suicide are low, this indicates that most people live by and accept local normative values. Conversely, where suicide rates are high (as in the France of his time), this indicates that "the collective" is failing to control and constrain "the individual." Durkheim also asserts that the individual human body is itself a social creation and possession. In Paris, Durkheim gathered around him a small cadre of thinkers who each elaborated this general view. Among them were Marcel Mauss, Henri Hubert, Robert Hertz, Lucien Levy-Bruhl, and others. The late British anthropologist E. E. Evans-Pritchard (1960) asserted that the analytical and theoretical writings of this group constituted the intellectual basis of modern social anthropology.

For Durkheim, the human body was the tabula rasa of social existence, the first "tool" of society itself, indeed, a living emblem of society. Paraphrasing Durkheim, Lock (1993) argues that social categories and norms are inscribed on and into the body, which, with prescriptions about body fluids, cosmetics, clothing, hair styles, depilation, and ornamentation, act as signifiers of moral worlds. Lock's use of the term *signifier* invites a brief comment. A construct or rule that signifies something can exist only in the context of a system of signs. By definition, signs are parts of symbol systems, which can be mediated, interpreted, and understood only with analytical intelligence (see Wolfe 1993). Although many animal species have vivid body parts and distinctive aromas, these have no meaning. They are merely signs, not symbols. Thus, in the Durkheimian view, the body is both figuratively and literally a living representation of society itself.

Building upon this tradition, that the individual is a product of the collective, Terrance Turner (1980) argues that the "social skin" is the common frontier between the individual and society at large. He asserts that the surface of the body is the stage upon which the drama of socialization is enacted. Body adornment, for example, is a form of language through which members of a society continually remind themselves, and tell others, who they *are* and who they are *not*. Comaroff (1985: 42) elaborates on this point with a slightly different emphasis:

> The relationship between the human body and the social collectivity is a critical dimension of consciousness in all societies. Indeed, it is a truism that the body is the tangible frame of selfhood in individual and collective experience, providing a constellation of physical signs with the potential for signifying the relation of persons to their context.

What this suggests, in short, is that our bodies are transformed within a matrix of cultural rules that allow us to read and therefore interpret and predict behavior. We are not really social beings until we are "read" or interpreted by some other person. Our physical and psychic being is dependent upon some kind of audience. We think we are who we are, but in reality we are our own interpretation of what *others* interpret us to be. Burridge (1979: 12) puts the matter this way: "We find and know ourselves only in what others say or do to us." As suggested earlier, what others say or do to us initially emerges in the serious matter of childhood play. The human body and human psyche are therefore not givens. They are more like an empty canvas that receive texture and form through cultural elaboration. When the mind and body are complete, they have been domesticated by a cultural formula (see also Benthall and Polemus, 1975; Blacking, 1977; Gilmore, 1994; Morinis, 1985; Polemus, 1978; Synnott, 1993; Wilson and Laennec, 1997).

RULES AND MEANINGS

Mary Douglas undertook graduate study in social anthropology in the early 1950s at Oxford University. At the time the Institute of Social Anthropology was under the direction of Evans-Pritchard, who, as noted above, was deeply influenced by Durkheim's sociological theory. Douglas carried out anthropological fieldwork among a people known as the Lele, who inhabit the upper regions of the Kasai River in the Democratic Republic of the Congo. Following this research, she went on to publish a range of articles on Lele belief and behavior. Into the 1960s, inspired in part by the ideas of her former graduate student colleague Franz Steiner, her anthropological interests took a more theoretical twist, and in 1966 she published the book *Purity and Danger,* a broadly comparative study of systems of symbolic classification.

In this study Douglas observes that people generally would rather live in a world in which they sense they have some control over day-to-day events than in a world of chaos and disorder. Worldviews or cosmologies provide a map of human experience and also rules to assure that this ordered view of life can be sustained. However, an ordered view of social experience will inevitably be confused or disrupted by one or another unexpected event. For example, most human beings are born alone. But sometimes twin births occur, creating an anomaly. Children are sometimes born with imperfectly formed genital organs, thus upsetting the norm that humans are born as clearly female or male. Douglas argues that one of the primary functions of ritual is to recognize, and then provide a means to deal with, such anomalies. In other words, ritual provides a way to reestablish cosmological order. In her terms, ritual provides a means to deal with *"matter out of place"* (emphasis added).

In this light a reasonable consequence is that the human body must also be subjected to a system of cultural control. The individual bodies that constitute a social system must be ordered or controlled in a manner that resonates with other cultural predispositions. As Douglas (1966) argues, controlling the human body is simultaneously a way of controlling society at large. Rules of body regulation and control are primary ways in which society is imposed upon us. Concurrently, transforming the body is a powerful symbol of this constraint.

Douglas examined these interpretations in further detail in her next theoretical text, *Natural Symbols* (1970; see also Mauss, 1936). She proposed a matrix through which one might predict how different forms of society impose and maintain codes of body control. This proposition is best understood in two different ways. The first entails an examination of some differences between two ideal types of social structure: mass society and face-to-face society. The second method is to examine a number of ethnographic cases in relation to hierarchy and social control.

FORMS OF SOCIAL LIFE

There are significant differences in the nature of social experience between densely populated, highly impersonal societies characteristic of the modern polyethnic nation-state and those that anthropologists have called kin-based, or face-to-face societies. In the first case, we walk through a major city amidst millions of other people and never make eye contact or even acknowledge the presence of another individual. Indeed, street sense dictates that initiating eye contact or conversation with a stranger can be life threatening. We eat meals in the company of total strangers and often don't know who has cooked the food. We might live for years in a densely populated apartment building and get by with but an occasional nod to the next-door neighbor. We live as strangers in a common culture. In this world we live under the constraints of thousands of laws though most of us are aware of only a small number of these. The general rule is "ignorance of the law is no excuse." Still, many live as though these laws have no personal relevance. If one can steal and not get caught, no problem. Nameless and faceless individuals feel no compelling need to adhere to any value system but their own. As we pass each other on the street, there is little if any accountability between us. And so, in Douglas's (1970) terms, arises the need for extreme body control. While we think we can do as we please and go where we want, growing ranks of police forces constantly monitor us. Many of our streets and roads are monitored by video cameras.

The contrasting situation is offered by kin-based or face-to-face societies. In such worlds it is not the case that rules are not broken or that individuals don't make their own choices. Rather, one finds here a greater density of common norms and values and, thus, a much higher degree of personal accountability. While my wife and I lived in the southern Sudan in the late 1970s, the vast majority of people we befriended had never, and would never, travel more than twenty miles from where they were born. People who first met in early childhood would be acquaintances until death. Although on paper it was part of the modern nation of Sudan, it was a world that had existed without standing armies or codified law. Virtually every adult could reckon some degree of kinship with almost everyone else, either through descent or marriage. The very basis of social life was the result of extensive sharing—of labor, of resources and of common values. Disputes were settled on the basis of particular circumstances and in deference to the valued reasoning of respected elders. Apart from a modest public covering for adult women and a string of beads or an ivory armband for men, the public body was subject only to informal control.

A far more extensive inventory of contrasts could be provided; however, Douglas's (1970) argument emerges clearly. The more people share in common the less they feel compelled to protect themselves from others. Conversely, the greater the degree of differentiation in a society, the more the body is subject to social control.

HIERARCHY AND THE BODY

Another way to elaborate Douglas's (1970) thesis is to consider the body in relation to a range of social practices and institutions that are based on extreme hierarchy and differential access to power. Hindu

India provides the most complete example of an entire society based on this principle. Brahmins are the most pure of castes, representing the "head" of society, while untouchables are the most impure—the feet of society, who recycle its wastes and impure products. The topic I want to address is not a society-wide form of hierarchy of the Hindu sort, but rather subsystems within single societies.

When a young Nuer of the southern Sudan attains adolescence, he will tell his father that it is time for his initiation into manhood through the ceremony known as *gar*. Nuer say that a young man must enter adulthood in the manner he was born. He and his age-mates are collected together in a public space. Their body hair is shaved and they are instructed to lie naked, backs to the ground. A ritual expert then cuts a parallel series of six deep incisions across their foreheads, beginning at the back of one ear and across to the other. This is an extremely painful procedure, and no medication is given to ease the trauma. They remain together in a hut for a month or so until their wounds have healed. Following this period of seclusion, they reemerge into public life and are given new names in light of their new social status. Among the Maasai of eastern Africa a different painful drama precedes the social declaration of male adulthood. Adolescent boys between the age of fourteen and fifteen years are circumcised in public as an age-set. They are held to the ground by adult men, legs spread apart, while ritual experts perform the operation. They struggle fiercely to free themselves and curse the man who cuts away at their most sensitive body part. They will become "true" men years later, after they have married and sired children.

These two brief ethnographic examples may be regarded in two different though complementary ways. First, each form of body transformation becomes a marker of ethnic identity, a topic discussed more fully in the next chapter. Second, in relation to Douglas's (1970) thesis, body transformation here functions as a means to establish and control political hierarchy. In each society, attaining socially defined adult status is possible only by suffering intense pain, inflicted by an older generation.

Closer to home, one can point to a number of situations in which hierarchy is also the basis of body control. The armed services provide an obvious example. Boot camp, or basic training, is at one and the same time a period of teaching and taunting. Perfectly made beds, perfectly shined shoes, and perfectly controlled bodies are all pieces of the same matrix. Indeed, it is in the nature of military hierarchy that the individual is totally subsumed by the system, since in the context of armed conflict the soldier's life is not subject to his or her own control. A different example is provided by Hodges (1997: 27), who notes that GIs entering service during World War II "were subjected to unannounced inspections of their penises, called a 'short arm' inspection. Soldiers with intact penises were declared phimotic [a condition where the foreskin cannot be retracted] and sent off to be circumcised, sometimes under the threat of court marshal." In the context of armed conflict, soldiers are awarded and promoted either for the number of human beings they kill or for the degree to which their own bodies have been maimed.

A closely analogous Western institution that mirrors the military quest for total body control is the penal system. Numbered rather than named and clad in identical uniforms, those deemed too dangerous to live in public society are likewise subjects of total body control. In recent Western history, those who were designated as "insane" were treated in the same manner.

Many other rigidly hierarchical organizations likewise impose their values onto the human body. Religious institutions often demand total control of the clergy and in doing so deny individuals bodily pleasures. In the monastic world, the monk's body was likewise under total institutional control, defining when he could eat, sleep, and even talk. For lay populations, periods of fasting, making pilgrimages, or experiencing trance are just are small number of ways in which religious values are imposed on the human body. For dedicated religious practitioners, such as Catholic nuns or priests, Hindu ascetics, or Buddhist monks, the body is under total control of religious strictures. One could argue, indeed, that one of the primary functions of religious ideology is the control of the human body. Modern corporate culture likewise entails a system of body control. "Casual Friday" aside, success in the corporate world entails devotion to the corporation through such customs as a rigid dress code, the expectation of extensive time commitment, and the possibility of urine or blood tests for substance abuse.

The following sections of this chapter draw upon ethnographic data relating to the human body and its transformation across the life cycle, from birth to death. Limitations of space preclude a comprehensive, cross-cultural discussion. Rather, I have drawn examples in order to emphasize the broad range of assumptions and usages found in different cultures regarding birth, sexuality, and death.

CULTURE AND BIOLOGY

Ideas relating to gestation and childbirth carry with them cultural as well as biological meanings. Where we are born, the first language we speak, what we are named, how our sexual and personal identity are formed, and what will happen to our bodies at death are all matters that are culturally determined. They are phenomena over which we have little if any control.

Society provides its members with a scheme or theory regarding gestation and heredity. In some cultures the newborn child is said to be the reincarnation of an ancestor and is thus a link in the unending process of creation and recreation. For Hindus, birth is said to be the consequence of behavior in a past life; it also promises the possibility of rebirth into a higher caste in a future life. Still other cultures posit a relationship between human birth and a totemic affiliation—the notion that there is a symbolic affinity between an animal species and a particular descent group. In such cases there is commonly a myth that suggests the founding ancestor of a clan was born as a twin with a totemic ancestor. Indeed, since totemic cosmologies are so widely reported in the ethnographic literature, it has been suggested that this form of symbolic logic makes a natural impression on the human imagination (see, e.g., Lévi-Strauss, 1966; Needham, 1980).

As for gestation, Socrates argued that if the child was born male, fertilization had occurred with semen from the right testicle and if female, from the left. A seventeenth-century scientist in France claimed to have seen under his microscope perfectly formed human beings inside sperm. Peoples of the Trobriand Islands became famous in the anthropological literature since they claimed no knowledge of the relationship between heterosexual intercourse and pregnancy. It was only in the late nineteenth century that our current understanding of gestation was fully formulated.

In the majority of the so-called "traditional" societies that anthropologists have studied, the birthing process itself is a singularly feminine occasion, although an interesting custom known as the couvade is practiced in a number of societies, particularly in Amazonian South America. In the practice of couvade, throughout the course of his wife's pregnancy, a husband complains of physical pain and discomfort, up to and even during the moment of birth. Anthropologists disagree over the meaning of the custom. Some have suggested that this is a form of symbolic domination or an expression of envy. Since men cannot give birth, they try to mimic and thereby control this uniquely female capability. Others have likened it more to masculine support for female pain and hardship, along the lines of the Lamaze birthing practice.

Culture makes its impact soon after birth. As Miller (1987, 1993, 1997) has revealed, in many areas of northern India the male baby has a much higher chance of living beyond the age of two than does a baby girl. Here, the birth of a male child is cause for celebration and is accompanied by ceremony and ritual. The birth of a daughter goes publicly unrecognized. Data that Miller collected from health clinics as well as interviews revealed that baby boys received far more medical attention in early infancy than did baby girls. It is reported for the Inuit of sub-Arctic Canada that on occasion, a mother will smother a daughter soon after birth. By limiting the number of potentially fertile women, the Inuit have come upon a means to assure that the human population will never outgrow available food resources.

While childbirth is obviously a female achievement and a biological fact, fatherhood is more subject to cultural definition and elaboration. Until recently in North America, a husband could only assume that he was the biological father of his wife's child. In many Western societies, a man places great value on the assurance that he is in fact the biological father of his children. In other cultures the matter of biological fatherhood appears less important than the establishment of legitimate social identity for the newborn. Two quite different ethnographic examples illustrate this fact.

Among various peoples of Nepal, anthropologists have studied a form of marriage called fraternal polyandry. Here, a woman is commonly married to two or three uterine brothers simultaneously. A wife determines the occasions of intimacy with her husband and also declares which of her husbands is the father of each of her children. There may or may not be a correlation between the social construction and the biological construction of the child. But in any case, the child will be born as legitimate.

Among the Atuot of the southern Sudan the cultural construction of birth can occur in a variety of forms. As is the case in many societies of sub-Saharan Africa, polygyny is common. A man may be married to as many women as he has resources to provide for. Atuot suggest that a primary reason for marriage is to produce children. As a cattle-herding people who also practice horticulture, the Atuot need large families to assure sufficient labor for economic tasks. From a woman's point of view children are also a kind of social security for needs in later life. Many adult women are widows late in life, and they rely on their children's help. For men, a large family assures that there will be sons to perpetuate their lineages and their social immortality.

Atuot men marry by the rule known as primogeniture: the eldest son of a family marries first, then his next-eldest brother, and so on. Should a man die before he had the opportunity to marry (and therefore have no sons to carry on his name and his lineage), his younger brother assumes the responsibility to marry a wife in his elder brother's name. In local usage, a woman is married to the "ghost" of the elder brother, and any children she bears will be called children of the dead man. The wife of the ghost may cohabit with any man she chooses, as long it would not be an incestuous relationship. Custom suggests that after she has borne three children in the name of the ghost, she may remarry, and the younger brother can then also seek his own wife. But it may also be the case that the second brother dies before his turn at marriage, in which case a third son inherits the responsibility to arrange a ghost marriage. Tracing "true" biological relationships in such circumstances can be well-nigh impossible. The Nepalese system of fraternal polyandry and the Atuot practice of ghost marriage do not deny that birth and gestation are natural processes. Rather, they suggest that the natural facts of childbirth are subject to extraordinary cultural manipulation.

BIRTHING CULTURE

The topic of birth and culture is vast. A growing literature on the topic is emerging (see, e.g., Corea, 1985; Davis-Floyd, 1992; Davis-Floyd and Sargent, 1997; Ford, 1964; Handwerker, 1993; Jordan, 1993; Kitzinger and Davis, 1978; Laderman, 1983; MacCormack, 1994; Mitford, 1992; Rapp, 1999; Rothman, 1982; Sargent, 1989; Whiteford and Poland, 1989; Winslow, 1980). Here I will discuss only two "cultures of birthing," one from a mass society and the other from a face-to-face society.

Davis-Floyd's monograph *Birth as an American Rite of Passage* (1992) was recognized as a classic study soon after its publication, and I have drawn from her observations primarily in the discussion that follows. It is at once a fine-grained analysis of the culture of American medical practice and also an exemplary study of ritual and rites of passage.

Beginning in the seventeenth century in the West, the human body came to be regarded less as natural creation of divine inspiration and more as an autonomous entity with the properties of a machine. According to Davis-Floyd, medical practice, too, was becoming a form of mechanical practice. Machines broke and mechanics fixed them. Improperly functioning bodies were likened to improperly working machines and had to be "fixed." In the technocratic, masculine world of medicine, pregnancy was increasingly regarded as a "condition" to be diagnosed and remedied by masculine science. David-Floyd (1992: 51) writes, "Obstetrics was thereby conjoined from its beginnings to develop tools and technologies for the manipulation and improvement of the inherently defective and therefore anomalous and dangerous process of birth." The social impact of this emerging practice was vast. Until the end of the nineteenth century most women in North America delivered their babies at home. By the 1940s, over 90 percent of North American women gave birth in hospitals.

In the hospital, Davis-Floyd suggests, a pregnant woman and her birthing tract are regarded as a birthing machine attended by able technicians working hard to meet production and quality control demands. She cites the remark of one intern to make her point: "'We shave 'em, we prep 'em, we hook 'em up to the IV and administer sedation. We deliver the baby, it goes to the nursery and the mother goes to her room. There's no room for niceties around here. We just move 'em on through'" (quoted in Davis-Floyd, 1992: 55). A production line, indeed—a descendant of a Detroit automobile factory. Davis-Floyd suggests that the concern is not for the birthing mother, but rather the perfection of a technique that will birth a perfect baby. The "natural" part of birth is entirely regulated, monitored and executed by a technocratic script. As she writes:

> This focus on the production of the perfect baby is a fairly recent development, a direct result of the combination of the technocratic emphasis on the baby-as-product with the new technologies available to assess fetal quality. Amniocentesis, ultrasonography, antepartum fetal heart stress, and intrapatern surveillance of fetal heart action, uterine contractions, and physiochemical properties of fetal blood are but a few of these new technologies. (57)

Soon after birth, the child is removed from its mother, placed in an artificial plastic womb, and its vital life signs are monitored. In this way, society symbolically demonstrates ownership of its product (Davis-Floyd, 1992: 58).

The popularity of Lamaze deliveries in the 1970s and 1980s seems to have peaked, and even while midwifery and home delivery have gained recent popularity, technology increasingly dominates birthing culture to the extent that it is ever more difficult to think of gestation and childbirth as anything natural at all. Semen and eggs are routinely frozen, advertised, and bought. Web sites now welcome bids for eggs produced by popular fashion models.

As a typical case, Davis-Floyd summarizes the procedure from arrival to the hospital to delivery. Upon entering the registration area, a woman is seated in a wheelchair, as though she was experiencing a medical "condition," and the taken to the "prep" room. Her clothes are removed, her pubic hair may be shaved, and she is given a vaginal examination, very often followed by an enema. Next, she is hooked up to an IV, and a pitocin drip is started to speed up the natural cycle of uterine contractions. A fetal monitor is strapped around her abdomen, and then an internal fetal monitor is attached to the baby's scalp. When birth seems imminent, she is wheeled to a delivery room, and her pubic area is doused with antiseptic. She is moved to a delivery chair lying at roughly a forty-five degree angle, so that her underside is immediately assessable to the attending physician. While in this position a nurse encourages her to bring on uterine contractions, even though she must now do so against the force of gravity. In most cases an episiotomy is performed: the doctor makes an incision between the vagina and the rectum. The medical rationale for this procedure is twofold: it lessens the likelihood that the vagina will tear during birth and also lessens stress on the baby's head during delivery. With the birth completed, assuming no other complications such as a breech birth, the need for a caesarian operation, or the use of high forceps, the placenta is removed, her episiotomy is sutured, and she is given another dose of pitocin to make her uterus contract.

Davis-Floyd (1992: 152) offers this interpretation:

> Although not all of the above procedures are performed on all moth-
> ers and babies, most of them are performed on most women most of
> the time. . . . They are patterned and repetitive; they are profoundly
> symbolic, communicating messages through the body, and the emo-
> tions, concerning our culture's deepest beliefs about the necessity
> for cultural control of natural processes, the untrustworthiness of
> nature, and the associated weakness and inferiority of the female
> body, the superiority of science and technology, and the importance
> of institutions and machines.

Recall Douglas (1970): faceless or mass societies produce extreme
measures to control the body. The preceding summary provides a decisive example of this. It contrasts starkly with birthing culture among
the Atuot of the southern Sudan. Here, the ethnographic summary is
considerably shorter since the process of childbirth in this society is
largely a personal rather than a public affair. Among the Atuot, a
woman typically delivers her child in the company of her mother and
another woman we would call a midwife. By custom, a woman gives
birth to her first child in her natal home. When her contractions begin,
she kneels over a cured cowhide mat in the middle of her mother's hut
and then begins to push while clenching a stick of wood in her mouth.
Once the child is born, she bathes it and offers it her breast. When she
later emerges from the hut, with her baby secure in a sling hanging
from her shoulder, her father, brothers and other natal kin will sacrifice
a goat or sheep to celebrate the event.

Human reproduction and birth are clearly natural, biological phenomena, but their form and meaning are highly regulated by distinctive cultural recipes.

THE BODY AND SOCIAL VALUES

The concluding chapter of this text examines current and emerging technology relating to the human body and some of the moral and
ethical questions they raise. Here, I focus on the ways cultural values
and morality are inscribed on the human body. Some of these have a
very public audience while others are more intimate.

For most people, during the second decade of life, secondary sex
characteristics emerge. Like birth and reproduction, this is a natural
process, but it is simultaneously under constant cultural monitoring.
Indeed, aspects of physical maturation have been notably altered by
cultural practices. By way of example, throughout the twentieth century in North America the age of first menstruation for girls has
decreased, likely in association with a changing diet. Conversely, it is

reported for a number of societies in the highlands of Papua New Guinea that sexual maturity for males and females comes rather late, at eighteen to twenty years. The local diet has also been cited as the dominant factor for this. The onset of adolescent sexuality is in any case a matter of universal cultural concern. Every human society gives recognition to this as a significant occasion, and every society attempts to control these natural processes in one way or another. Thus, like most other aspects of our biosocial being, sexuality is also culturally constructed and controlled. Social, rather than natural, facts establish when we are sexually mature, when it is permissible to engage in sexual behavior, who are proper sexual partners, as well as the age that reproductive behavior should begin. Human beings engage in more nonreproductive sexual behavior than virtually any other species (Bonobo chimps and two-toed sloths beat us here.) It is no surprise, therefore, that human sexuality is constantly constrained by cultural values and norms. My concern here is not with sexuality or sexual behavior, but with the cultural control of this behavior.

A brief review of North American medical practice clearly demonstrates the close relation that exists between social values, morality, and the human body. (It is important to remember that our culture grew out of remarkably different traditions, some that were native and others that were imported.) By the middle of the nineteenth century, various regionalisms aside, cultural orthodoxies took form. According to Hodges:

> Orthodox American medicine had embarked on the wholesale amputation of the sexual organs as a cure for seemingly unrelated diseases. Insane asylums castrated inmates on a massive scale to prevent their masturbating and, ostensibly, to cure their insanity. Up until the turn of the last century, boys who were caught masturbating were frequently committed to insane asylums, castrated, and shackled to their cells. Females were likewise subjected to female castration, a surgery involving the removal of the ovaries, with the intent of curing them of hysteria, epilepsy, or nymphomania. Clitoridectomy was commonly practiced. (1997: 22; see also Bryk, 1934)

Indeed, a Dr. Sayre (see Hodges, 1997: 28) delivered a paper at the 1870 meeting of the American Medical Association where he proved to the evident satisfaction of his audience that the foreskin of the penis was not only the cause of paralysis but also hip-joint disease, hernia, poor digestion, inflammation, and general clumsiness. He asserted that after he had performed circumcisions on patients with these conditions, they soon recovered.

In a following paper Sayre (see Hodges, 1997: 23) argued that female circumcision (specifically, the excision of the clitoris) cured paralysis of the bladder, curvature of the spine, and club feet. M. J. Moses (see Hodges, 1997: 23), a colleague of Sayre, suggested in an article in the

New York Medical Journal in 1895 that male circumcision should become established practice in order to inhibit masturbation, and by 1914 (see Hodges, 1997: 25) an editorial in the *Journal of the American Medical Association* asserted that it was every physician's moral duty to circumcise young children. In 1965 Dr. K. C. Morgan debunked the myth about the values of male circumcision in an essay appropriately titled "The Rape of the Phallus," also published in this prestigious journal.

Hodges (1997: 36; see also De Meo, 1997; Stead, 1999) offers a summary of North American medical practice attending this operation:

> The historical record makes it clear that physicians institutionalized the sexual mutilation of children as a means of attempting to eradicate childhood sexuality. . . . Whatever incurable disease happens to be in the focus of national attention in any given time period will be the disease that circumcision advocates will use as an excuse for circumcision:
>
> 1870s: for epilepsy, circumcision
> 1940s: for sexually transmitted diseases, circumcision
> 1950s: for cancer, circumcision
> 1980s: for AIDS, circumcision
>
> This unscientific allegiance to a perpetually ineffective, radical and prejudicial surgical procedure corroborates the hypothesis that there is a deeper, non-rational, psychosexual dynamic behind circumcision advocacy.

This commentary is important for two reasons. First, members of Western cultures tacitly assume that their customs are rational, logical, coherent, and in the best sense of the term, "modern." We have science, which has freed us from irrationality, ignorance, and bias. These practices and assumptions would suggest otherwise. And thus the second point: it is a fundamental truth of anthropological method and practice that there is irrationality in *all* human endeavors, in any society, at any point in time.

Sexuality is a powerful symbol in all societies. By comparison with other practices, however, the Western form of male genital modification is rather mild. Well into the last century it was common for men in Yemen and parts of Saudi Arabia to have all of the skin covering the penis removed. Penal subincision was common practice in numerous societies of Melanesia and Australia. In numerous societies of Southeast Asia the penis pin is a common element of material culture. Here, the glans of the penis is pierced from one side to the other, and a brass rod with beaded ends is inserted. From the local perspective, the practice is cited as a means to enhance aesthetic beauty and to increase female pleasure during intercourse.

A topic much in the media of late is the phenomenon known as female circumcision, or clitoridectomy, which some consider female genital mutilation. Society's probing into the most intimate and sensitive part of a woman's body surely begs some explanation, as does the cultural alteration of intimate male anatomy.

As noted previously, female circumcision was common practice in postcolonial North America, and there are good reasons to suspect that it was equally common in nineteenth-century Europe. In the contemporary world, clitoridectomy is most widely reported in the Islamic world, although the practice is not codified in any sacred Islamic scripture or text. That is, while it is common in many Muslim societies, *it is not called for* by Islamic faith. Indeed, the practice is also common in a number of societies of eastern Africa, even where there is no allegiance to Islam, as well as among many peoples of non-Muslim western Africa, who perform the act as a matter of religious devotion.

Clitoridectomy does not refer to a single type of genital transformation. The excision of the clitoris is not a universal procedure in the cultural transformation of female genitalia. Instead, the operation varies from removing some of the external labia and the tip of the clitoral hood to the radical or pharaonic form, which entails the surgical removal of all labial skin as well as the entire clitoris. Among the Maasai of Tanzania and Kenya, the Gikuyu of Kenya, the Islamic peoples of the Sahel region of Africa, and the Swahili peoples of coastal eastern Africa, milder forms are the norm. A female colleague of mine who had lived among the Turkana of northern Kenya related the following story. She learned that Turkana women circumcise their daughters shortly before the onset of puberty. Her female friends were astonished and aghast—and somewhat disgusted—when they learned that this was not common practice in North America. But, my anthropological friend asked, how was it when you had sex with your husband? Turkana women replied, "It's always good having sex with your husband."

From a Western perspective, this particular form of body transformation is typically alleged to be repressive and dehumanizing. In its most radical form, female circumcision can and does create life-threatening complications from inflammation and infection and excessive bleeding, not to mention emotional and psychological wounds. The most comprehensive and insightful anthropological monograph on the topic was written by the Canadian anthropologist Janice Boddy (1989) in a work titled *Wombs and Alien Spirits*. Her study focused on women living in a small rural village along the banks of the White Nile, a day or so by public transport to the north of Khartoum, the capital of Sudan. Like many small towns in the Islamic world, Hofyriat (the pseudonym she chose to call it) is surrounded by mud walls, and each homestead within it is secluded from the next by a high wall, with only a single doorway that opens to the street and the outside world. In a very general sense, Boddy found, village residents felt separated from the outside world around them and therefore also a need for protection from the larger world. Women's bodies, she argues, are living metaphors of this cultural concern—a desire to be closed off from intrusions of the outside world. And thus, like the village itself, a woman's body must be closed to unwanted and potentially threatening invasions. From this perspective, Boddy interprets the local theory of the female body.

Her ethnographic representation is fine-grained and locally informed. To adult Hofyriat women, the female body must be culturally controlled and secured; this necessity provides their rationale for performing pharaonic circumcision. A "sealed" body is safe from foreign intrusion, and to the extent that the women of the village are safe from external threats, so too is the village. Prior to a young girl's clitoridectomy, her body is bathed and then "smoked" with aromas from burning herbs and other fragrant substances. All of her body hair is removed, and then an adult woman quickly slices away the labia and clitoris, and after leaving a small opening through which menstrual blood and urine can be eliminated, sews the wound together. Her legs are then bound to limit blood loss after the operation. The operation is followed by celebration, song, dance, and feasting. This is a moment of great pride for the girl's mother and other close female relatives—the culmination of all the time, patience, loving, and teaching that it takes to turn a girl into a woman. Now she is protected from the outside world and its potential dangers. Later in life, when she is married, the small opening will be surgically enlarged to allow for intercourse and, eventually, childbirth. After the birth of her child, she will be resewn. And so it goes until she experiences menopause.

Even while intimate sexual behavior lies at the foundation of the reproduction of society, sexuality appears at the same time to threaten the possibility of orderly, rule-governed social existence. Recalling Douglas (1970) again, because sexuality is so powerful, it is inherently dangerous. As she argued in *Purity and Danger*, anything that is dangerous and threatening to the social order is bounded by ritual control and prohibition. It is hardly surprising, in this light, that the cultural transformation of the sexual body occurs during the early, formative years of life and that society imparts these messages in deliberate, often painful ways. Controlling sexuality and the body is a primary means of ordering society itself. It is society, rather than its individual members, that defines and determines what we do with our seemingly intimate selves. The sexual life of the body is very much a part of the social life of the body.

THE SOCIAL LIFE OF HAIR

If our most intimate body parts bear the stamp of culture, so too do our more overtly public selves, an observation that can be elaborated through a consideration of the social significance and manipulation of body hair. This is a topic that has attracted considerable anthropological attention. As noted in the preceding chapter, in the course of evolution, human activity and invention altered the distribution of hair on the body. The use of fire and the eventual use of clothing usurped nature's plan for keeping us warm. Head hair persists, as noted earlier, as a means to protect the brain from excessive heat, and the growth of tufts of hair elsewhere on the body signal the onset of sexual maturity. Clearly, as a natural facet of the human body, hair has no self-evident "meaning." Hair is another aspect of the natural human body that is everywhere under cultural control. As the anthropologist O. Obeyesekere (1998: xii) writes, "hair is by itself not a natural symbol but one that provokes the work of culture."

The Freudian psychologist Charles Berg (1951), who wrote a book titled *The Unconscious Significance of Hair*, in fact inspired the anthropological appreciation of body hair. In Berg's view, the manipulation of head hair is symbolic of genital manipulation: what is done to head hair represents the psychosexual orientation of the individual person. In this view, the cutting or removal of head hair is a symbolic expression of castration, asexuality, or a public expression of deference to external, extrapersonal authority and power. Military and corporate customs provide ready examples of this. By the same reasoning, uncontrolled head hair is a symbol of untempered and aggressive sexuality and freedom from social constraints. The tendency of rock stars to elaborate this theme provides an apt and counterexample to the military ritual.

In response to this personally oriented interpretation, the late British anthropologist Edmond Leach (1958) wrote an essay that was published in 1958 in the *Journal of the Royal Anthropological Institute* titled "Magical Hair." Leach's primary rebuttal to Berg's thesis was that body hair is an inherently public rather than private phenomenon and therefore invited a cultural rather than individual or psychological interpretation. Grooming body hair, Leach argued, was in fact just another way in which cultural norms constrain individual behavior and identity. About a decade later Hallpike (1969) joined the debate to argue that "hair behavior" had less to do with psychological phenomena and more to do with the perennial dialogue between the individual and society at large. Hallpike took his stance on the basis of comparative ethnography. Religious ascetics often have long and unkempt hair, even while their religious devotions proscribe sexuality. Long hair therefore does not necessarily, or always, denote ribald sexuality. Similarly, in many and diverse societies, custom dictates that after the death of a person, kin and friends should mark the occasion by letting their body hair, and particularly head hair, grow as it will, a notion that is also quite often accompanied by a sustained period of sexual abstinence. In Hallpike's view, long hair is polysemous—simultaneously symbolizing numerous things—such as temporarily being beyond the strictures of social life, of rejecting social norms. The essential argument here is that hair is a medium of public discourse and not simply a matter of personal, unconscious symbolism.

The anthropological dialogue on this topic then moved on to a debate about "religious hair" (Duncan 1973) and then a consideration of "hair, sex, and dirt" (Hershman 1974). That human body hair has great symbolism at both the personal and collective level is a well-established ethnographic fact. That its meaning varies cross-culturally is equally apparent. That it is regulated by culture is beyond question. Another obvious fact invites emphasis: hair has both psychological and social meaning. One particular theoretical stance on the issue is no more compelling than the other.

In many cultures, long, unkempt body hair serves as a symbol of the natural, or wild world. When I was living among the Atuot of the southern Sudan, children delighted in sneaking up behind me to pluck hair from my legs while shouting "Lion! Lion!" In this culture, hairiness is associated with the wild, uncontrolled and threatening world of the forest, and the removal of all body hair is regarded as a normal practice of personal hygiene and body aesthetics. Men carefully pluck their beards, and women make a paste out of honey to remove their body hair. Adults let their hair grow long only as a public expression of mourning, a common tradition in many African societies. It is in fact a common theme of human cultures that the control of body hair is a way of emphasizing the distinction between the world of humans and the world of animals (cf. Berman, 1999).

Some time ago Cooper (1971) pointed out that whereas head hair is a widely desired embellishment, body hair is subject to considerable cultural elaboration. In ancient Egypt, women and men removed all body hair, which was thought to be both ugly and unhygienic. Likewise, in ancient Greece, women regularly rid their bodies of pubic hair. Greek custom had its influence on Roman civilization, and Roman women followed similar practices. Turkish women shaved their pubic hair and decorated their labia with henna (Cooper, 1971: 85). In the Middle Ages, returning Crusaders brought back the Arab idea of pubic depilation for women, and this became the dominant fashion for the European aristocracy at the time (114). In fifteenth-century France it became "elegant custom" for women to be completely free of body hair. Bouhdiba (1988: 203) has commented on this practice for women in the Islamic world:

> So the female sex is particularly loved when it is hairless. Indeed, the fact is that depilation is an important element in the practices of the *hammam* [bath] of hygiene, of the art of making oneself beautiful and ready for sexual activity. . . . Hairiness is anti-erotic and indeed only young girls and women in mourning are released from the obligation to shave pubic hair and depilate the body. An unshaven vagina is readily compared to the evil eye.

In many contemporary Islamic societies, the phrase "going to the *hammam*" is a euphemism for "going to make love," since bathing and the shaving of the arms, the legs, and lastly the pubic area are also preparations for sexual relations. Indeed, the removal of pubic hair is part of the *Hadith,* or religious tradition (Bouhdiba, 1983: 33–34).

Similar practices are certainly in evidence in our own society. Full body waxing and laser hair removal are increasingly popular techniques of cosmetic culture. Indeed, the "hair culture" of North America is a multibillion-dollar industry. The cultural control and transformation of body hair is one of the most obvious and one of the most powerful ways in which our individual selves take social form. The cultural manipulation of body hair communicates information not only about gender and sexuality but also about ethnic identity, religious affiliation, social and economic status, as well as age. The language of body hair is surely a means of self-expression, but it is also a way in which we are marked and transformed as culture-bearing creatures (see also Barkan, 1975; Berthelot, 1986; ; Brochdue, 1993; Bynum, 1971; Ebin, 1979; Gaines and Herzog, 1990; Laquer, 1968; Levine, 1995; Mageo, 1994; Napolitan, 1939; O'Halon, 1989; Sanders, 1989; Schilder, 1950; Sydie, 1987; Turner, 1984). It is simultaneously a part of the social life of the body that sends distinct messages between us from birth, through adulthood, and until death.

THE SOCIAL CONSTRUCTION OF DEATH

We've all seen the bumper sticker: life's a bitch, and then you die. We are not born into meaningless worlds; nor is death in any human society an uncontemplated "natural" fact. Just as we are formed into particular kinds of human beings through birth and socialization, so too do we leave this world in culturally constructed ways. The human body is no more free of cultural elaboration at birth than it is at death. Indeed, dying itself is a fundamental part of the social life of the body.

Simply stated, death is something we have to learn rather than something we naturally do. I recall a personal anecdote. I'd guess I wasn't more than five years old at the time, visiting my maternal grandmother's small dairy farm in northern New Hampshire. It was

about 5:30 in the afternoon when I was told to go into the barn to tell
Tildon, my grandmother's second husband, that it was time to come
into the house for dinner. Off to the barn I went. It seemed enormous to
me at the time—a huge loft with deep layers of hay to play in, six or
seven stalls, with a horse and milking cows. Tildon was lying on the
aged and creaking wooden floor with a pitchfork in his hand. This
immediately struck me as odd: why would he be lying on the floor of the
barn to take a nap? I called to him, "Tildon, it's time to wake up for dinner." I was very frightened: Tildon was a very old man to me, and I
really didn't know him well. He didn't move, so I guessed he must be
really tired. Waking him up was a job for an adult. I walked back into
the kitchen and announced to my grandmother and parents that Tildon
was taking a nap in the barn and wouldn't wake up. There was a sud-
den flurry of movement as the three adults rushed down the hall and
into the barn. Kneeling next to his body, my grandmother announced
that Tildon was dead. At age five, I reasoned that being dead simply
meant being a different kind of sleeping. While death is a natural fact,
it has meaning only as a culturally constructed event.

The Hindu ascetic performs his own funeral rites as part of his
(most are men) initiation into this holy status. From then on, he lives
like a wandering ghost. Unlike his fellow secular humans, upon death,
his corpse is not cremated, but simply deposited in the Ganges River.
He is socially dead at the very moment he becomes an ascetic (see Bloch
and Parry, 1982). The late anthropologist Evans-Pritchard reported an
oddly similar circumstance for the Nuer of the southern Sudan. Normally, in Nuer society, the situation of death is marked by the act of animal sacrifice. Nuer are highly concerned that the ghost of a deceased
person may linger among the living and cause misfortune. On this occasion Nuer will say, "Now you ghosts, you are finished with us, you are
the people of God, you are the people on the other side" (Evans-Pritchard, 1956: 152). But Evans-Pritchard also learned of another man
who was physically alive, but socially dead:

> There was living in a village in western Nuerland an unhappy-look-
> ing man of unkempt appearance named Gatbough. This man had
> some years before gone on a distant journey and had not been heard
> of for a long time. Then there came to his village news of his death
> and in the course of time the mortuary ceremony was held for him.
> He later returned home and was living in the village at the time of
> my visit. He was described as the living ghost. . . . I was told his soul
> was cut off. His soul went with the soul of the sacrificed ox together.
> His flesh alone remains standing. His soul, the essential part of
> him, had gone and with it his social personality. Although people
> fed him, he seems to have lost his privileges of kinship. . . . A neigh-
> bor said to me "he lives in our village with Barayai but we do not
> count him as a member of it because he is dead. The mortuary cer-
> emony has been held for him." (152–153)

Whatever the locally constructed meaning of death, and whatever the ritual and ceremonial that attends it, the human corpse is the last stage on which the social drama of life is enacted. For many societies of Southeast Asia, the practice of secondary burial is reported: here, the body is buried not once, but twice, the first time so that flesh and body fluid will decompose and the second time to inter skeletal remains. Cremation of the corpse is common in many Asian and Melanesian societies, while funerary custom in North America is a multimillion-dollar industry, carefully monitored and regulated by state and federal statutes. Here, it is the state rather than individuals that determines where burials and cremations can occur as well as who has the legitimate authority and status to carry out the process (Mitford, 1992). Once interred, the deceased bodies of prominent social and political figures often become shrines of national, patriotic, and religious identity. St. Paul's Cathedral, the eternal flame in the Arlington National Cemetery, and the walls of the Kremlin are some of the most obvious examples, in addition to the thousands of shrines for local saints and deities throughout the world, to which the faithful make regular pilgrimage.

And thus ends the social life of the body: at the culmination of a prolonged series of ritual transformations that define and legitimize the individual body as a cultural entity. In this chapter I have attempted to develop and explicate Durkheim's concept that the body is itself a social fact and that it is ever at the interface between our sense of self-identity and our socially constructed sense of self. The human body is treated as an image of the society that produces it, and there can be no natural way to consider the body that does not simultaneously entail this social and cultural dimension. Concurrently, the physical experience of the body, always modified by the social categories through which it is known, sustains a particular image of that society (Douglas, 1970: 93), a matter that I examine in greater detail in the following chapter.

Chapter Three

Us and Them
Ethnicity, Identity, and the Body

The more similar people become, the more they have to stress their differences. (Steiner, 1999: 231)

When my son was four years old, he spent hours watching the popular movie *Dances with Wolves*. Of course at that age, he could not read the English subtitles that translated the Native American dialog, so I would translate for him. On one occasion he was clearly very troubled by the way soldiers treated the "Indians." I tried to explain a little about what happened when "white people" started to settle in the western part of North America. After listening for a few minutes, he turned to me and asked in a *very* concerned way, "Daddy, are *we* white people?"

One of the key strategies for survival in human prehistory was living in social groups. As a consequence of this, there arose numerous specializations of our increasingly complex brain: the ability to remember personal names, to recognize different faces, to feel compassion and emotion toward other human beings, and having a need to belong. Being "someone" really means being with others. The sense of "belonging" is learned early in childhood. Personal and ethnic identity emerges hand in hand with self-identity. In this chapter I review a number of ways in which the body serves as a vehicle for collective as well as ethnic identity. First, it is important to clarify the popular confusion between the terms "race" and "ethnicity."

THE MYTH OF RACE

In popular English the terms race and ethnicity are often used as though they were synonymous. In North America a common sentiment is that people who look different are members of a different "race." By the turn of the last century, Western science had in fact constructed elaborate schemes to classify and sort seemingly different "human races" with terms such as Caucasoid, Negroid, and Mongoloid. Although the ancient Greeks regarded certain peoples as socially inferior and thus thought of them as natural slaves, racial theory *in its modern form* largely arose in the context of Darwinian evolutionary theory. The term *race* entered the popular lexicon of English during the decades of European colonialism and imperialism—that moment in world history when it was asserted that it was the "white man's burden" to civilize "savage races." Prior to this time, European explorers more often referred to the local peoples they encountered in less prejudicial terms, such as the Iroquois nation, or the kingdom of Benin.

Anthropologists now widely recognize that the popular concept of race fundamentally confuses physical differences and cultural bias. That people differ in physical form is obvious; however, physical differences in the human form have nothing at all to do with ethnicity or culture. The concept race, when used to describe human biological difference, has absolutely no scientific validity. Like the term *species*, race refers to a population that can successfully interbreed and thus reproduce. There is therefore *one* category of humanity: the *human* race. Race is a cultural concept, not a natural fact.

That we inherit a genetic endowment is a biological given; yet virtually everything we do with it is mediated by culture. The next time someone mentions to you that he or she is one-quarter Irish, German, or Italian, ask the person *what* part: Their ears? Part of their feet? The basic confusion here originates in the misconception that we inherit identity "in our blood." This notion is likewise a residue of nineteenth-century racism, which posited a causal relationship between race, language, and culture. More than sixty years ago Julian Huxley (1941: 126) wrote, "It would be highly desirable if we could banish the question-begging term of 'race' from all discussions of human affairs and substitute the non-committal phrase ethnic group." During the period in which Huxley wrote, so-called "mixed marriages" were either void, illegal, or punishable as felonies in at least thirty states in America.

The mistaken notion that culture or ethnic identity is passed on by blood is well illustrated by legislation of 1927 in the American state of Georgia. The statute outlawed the marriage of a white person to anyone who was not "white." White people were those who had no ascertainable trace of Negro, African, West Indian, Asian, Indian, Mongolian, Japanese or Chinese blood in their veins (see Montague, 1942: 190). The bizarre notion that cultural identity is inherited by blood has been a key factor in the recognition of Native American ethnic identity, and it persists in a multitude of government documents. Many government forms ask for data regarding "racial" identity, such as African or Asian American. On the one hand, these are socially constructed categories. On the other hand, they are so vague as to be entirely meaningless. Asian-American? Let's see: that would include peoples from Turkey, India, Iran, most of the former Soviet Union, Thailand, Malaysia, the Philippines, Japan, China, to mention only a few countries—and nothing about the multitude of different cultures and languages within each. Asia is home to more than 2 billion human beings. As an ethnic category it is void of any specific meaning.

Although the phrase *ethnic group* is somewhat more desirable that the term *race*, it is also problematic because of its implicit presumption of a singular and timeless identity. Ethnic identity, like cultural identity, is not something we are born with. Rather, it is something we learn, and like language, ethnic identity is a phenomenon that is constantly in the process of change. Cultural and ethnic occasions and traditions are invented.

With these matters addressed briefly, it becomes clear that the terms *ethnicity* and *culture* share common meanings, but a distinction should be emphasized. It is useful to think of ethnicity as a way of acting out—or doing—culture. Our ethnic behavior is a three dimensional manifestation of culture: how we walk, how we talk, how and what we eat, and more generally, how we live through our cultural values and ideals.

As noted in the preceding chapter, a fundamental requisite for any society is the establishment of a means to enculturate and socialize its members. In the simplest terms, this occurs because local custom is represented as the unquestioned norm. From birth, individual psychologies develop amidst the context of local social psychologies. Child training is the particular cultured way of organizing experience. The emergence of identity entails a consistent sameness within oneself and a persistent sharing some kind of essential character with others. Much of this learning is mediated by the human body. As Isaacs (1995: 46–48) observes:

> The body is the most palpable element of which identity—individual or group—is made. . . . The body is at once the most intimate and inward, and most obvious outward aspect of how we see ourselves, how we see others, and how others see us. . . . More than anything else, physical characteristics seem as a badge of identity, instantly establishing who are the we and who are the they.

Shilling (1993: 12) gives this view a slightly different twist in suggesting that "the body is most profitably conceptualized as an unfinished biological and social phenomenon which is transformed as a result of its entry into, and participation, in society." The single most important process this entails is the mastery of language, since it is through language that the child discovers a particular view of the world. The mind and body are thus fashioned simultaneously.

THE ETHNICITY OF NAMES

One of the most obvious and utilitarian functions of language is the denotation of names for *things*—culturally constructed artifacts. Many anthropologists learning a foreign language in the course of fieldwork have had the tedious experience of collecting word lists—the local lexicon—in order to be able to speak as well as a local two-year old. Our hosts have often been gracious by ignoring our efforts in this task. In all human languages there is a distinctive set of terms that refer to people rather than objects: personal names. Personal names form a special grammatical class and are often based on metaphor and other symbolic references. The creation of the personal name is the first, and surely one of the most important, means by which ethnic identity is established.

As a start to this section one might first consider the broader realm of ethnic names, a topic that invites a separate in-depth study. Many peoples throughout the world have inherited ethnic designations that have been imposed upon them by strangers. In North America the most infamous example is *Indian*, a term that gained currency after Columbus's journeys. Indian then became a catchall phrase used by Europeans to refer to all Native Americans, thus ignoring (and denying) their considerable cultural diversity. Another well-known case of mistaken ethnic identity is provided by the term *Eskimo*. The term originated among Athabaskan speakers (such as the Cree of central Canada) and means "eaters of raw flesh." Athabaskan speakers reported to European travelers and missionaries that people who ate raw flesh lived to the north of their country. A common "Eskimo" term for self-reference is Inuit, meaning "the most civilized people in the world." Most indigenous ethnic names typically mean, "we are the only true people." It is impossible to imagine an Inuit woman or man approaching a foreigner and declaring, "Welcome to our home. We are the eaters of raw flesh." The Eastern African people known as Sukuma provide a parallel example. Early European explorers, some seeking the source of the White Nile, encountered a people called Nyamwezi, living to the east of Lake Tanganyika. When asked who lived to the north of their country Nyamwezi responded, "sukuma," a word in their language that means "the people who live to the north." Similar examples abound in the ethnographic literature.

Like many other aspects of human culture, personal names initially appear arbitrary. But the fact that naming is a universal dimension of human culture points to our need to be distinctly and discretely
recognized. The personal name is a key marker of personal and cultural
identity. While given at birth, personal names often change across the
life cycle, and in the process, we typically accumulate a number of
"nick" or "other" names. On occasion, we encounter others who share
our exact personal name, and the experience is unsettling. The personal name immediately identifies one as a member of a particular ethnic group or as a strange and foreign "other."

Clyde Kluckhon (see Burton, 1982) wrote that among the Navaho,
small children are not given personal names since kinship terms are sufficient at this point in life. It is only when the child begins to move more
independently in the public realm that a personal name is assigned;
Kluckhon found the naming system one of the most complex aspects of
Navaho culture. In learning about personal nomenclature among the
Penan of Southeast Asia, the anthropologist Rodney Needham must
have initially encountered similar difficulty, since here a person often
accumulates tens and even hundreds of personal and "nick" names.
Among the Akwe-Shavante of Brazil, a child isn't named for five to six
years for fear it may not survive infancy. Among the Mapuche of Chile,
birth is celebrated with a naming ceremony, which is intended to symbolically conjoin the living with deceased ancestors. Karp (see Burton,
1982) observes that among the Iteso of Kenya, the "sucking name" is the
one by which a child will be known throughout life. A short while following birth, a grandparent dips a finger into a pot of beer, places it in the
child's mouth and calls out a name that has been chosen. If the child
refuses to swallow, another name is selected, until the child swallows the
beer and thus accepts the name. Ocholla-Ayayo (see Burton, 1982)
observes for the Luo of Kenya that the personal name is as much a part
of a man's being as his soul and body.

For the Atuot of the southern Sudan (see Burton, 1982) the personal name is likewise an important marker of individual and social
identity. The Atuot verb "to name" *(cak)* is identical to the verb "to create." Typically the first-born child is named after the color of an ox or
cow that was part of the bridewealth settlement leading to marriage.
The local explanation is that the name not only identifies the child but
also serves as a record of the settlement of the marriage and, by extension, the wider group of people who attended the ceremony. A woman's
other children are named in association with some event ongoing at the
time of birth. A girl may be named *Nyuot*, indicating that she was born
during a heavy rainstorm. The name *Acok* relates that the child was
born during a period of famine. A friend had named his third son *Meth-
alek*. As he explained, a British agricultural consultant had been in the
area to introduce a new strain of groundnuts. The individual con-

cerned, a Mr. Lek, was recalled in this case since my friend's son was born as this crop was being harvested.

Most anthropologists have had the experience of being renamed by friends in the course of fieldwork. In our case, living among the Atuot, "John" simply didn't work. I was given as a first name *Mayan,* since the color of my skin was likened to the common cow color *mayan.* My second name, or "father's" name, was *Anginy,* the name of a man who had died three generations before and who had been a member of my adoptive lineage. Atuot assert that when deceased ancestors learn that a living person has been named in their memory, they will be pleased and therefore unlikely to harm the living. My wife's experience was somewhat different, but also informative. The first issue was the status of our marriage. While we claimed to be married, we had no children to prove the fact. Initially friends suggested I should marry an Atuot woman who could have children. Then we were asked how many cows were given as bridewealth in our marriage. I tried to explain that we exchanged "vows" and not cows. We had exchanged rings, not cows. To most this was still unacceptable. Then a man asserted, "You must be like the Arabs then. How much did you pay for your wife?" After some further discussion it was resolved that my wife's name would be *Alak,* the color of Sudanese paper currency. The underlying issue was an inability to understand how we could have been married without exchanging anything of value. From the local point of view, money must have been exchanged to establish the marriage, so the color of money would be her name.

Closer to home, our everyday encounter with names is a constant mirror of ethnic identity. During the early twentieth century, tens of thousands of immigrants had their names changed by officials at Ellis Island, New York, in a concerted effort to standardize emerging North American society and culture. In fact, many immigrants were eager to call their newborn children by English names, as a conscious effort to blend into this new society. A change in name was a simple way to transform ethnic identity. In contemporary North America, abuzz with discussions about multiculturalism, distinctive personal names have become fashionable badges of ethnicity. By example, Diego or Shakina clearly send a different message about cultural identity than Tom or Mary.

BODY SENSE

We are all born into a society that includes an ideal image of the human body—a body aesthetic. The bodies that we see create a template for recognizing a "normal" body. Some studies that have appeared in the recent media suggest that there are universal "ideal type" body forms. A careful reading of world ethnography suggests otherwise.

Rather, what is universal is the social convention to conform to a *particular* body aesthetic, basic to a common ethnic identity. On the whole, we feel more at ease in the company of people whose public bodies resemble our own. Isaacs (1995: 63) has even suggested that "The body is the most primordial of all features of basic group identity. . . . Extraordinarily powerful taboos and sanctions have been attached in many groups against exogamous unions or marriages that threaten their physical sameness." Although the custom of arranged marriage is foreign to Western societies, there is a tacit rule of class endogamy. We tend to marry individuals who come from a socioeconomic background similar to our own. That means we often marry people *who look like us*.

Bruce and Young (1998) have published a detailed study on factors affecting the perception of the human face (see also Bell, 1844; Bull and Rumsey, Darwin, 1872; Landau, 1989, 1988; Ligget, 1974). Recall that some of the particular characteristics of the human face are the consequence of enlarging skulls and brains in the course of human evolution. Bruce and Young (1998: 4) write:

> These general and species-specific factors mean that all human faces are remarkably similar in basic form. Despite this, there are subtle differences that make every face unique, so that faces play an important role in the identification of individuals in our highly social species, and systematic variations of the human face pattern inform us about mood, age, and sex.

Of course the face is also the most public sign of ethnic and cultural affiliation. Bruce and Young's (1990) study confirms what we intuitively know: we are attracted to faces that register with our particular cultural scheme, and individuals who are thought to be attractive amass social advantages (119–130). Bruce and Young also surmise that the recognition of human faces is of greater significance than the recognition and memory of personal names (185). Here one sees again the significance of the body as a marker of cultural and ethnic identity. If someone's external appearance resembles one's own, they are "one of us." That our brains are "hard-wired" to do this is evidenced by the condition known as prosopagnosia—the loss of the ability to recognize and identify human faces.

BODY IMAGES

The most obvious way in which the body serves as a marker of ethnic identity is the way in which it is transformed, either permanently by markings and scars of one form or another or by the "second skin" we don as a matter of cultural habit. However, we must learn a cultural grid to focus on what is most significant in the recognition of "ourkind" and others. Three distinct ethnographic examples amplify this point.

The first example to illustrate my point is provided by the encounter between the Spanish and the peoples of the New World. Against the orders of his commanding officer in Spanish Cuba, Hernando Cortes and his fleet of eleven ships arrived at Veracruz on the Gulf Coast of Mexico in 1519. Rumor current at the time suggested that in the interior of Mexico was a great empire resplendent with gold—the conquistadors' constant craving. Many historians have written masterful texts on the events that led to the eventual conquest of Mexico, but few have addressed the following fact at length. None of the indigenous people of Mexico knew what they were seeing upon first contact with Cortés and his armies. How strange indeed: here were creatures with humanlike faces, but with heads and bodies of a bright shiny material and one arm that was flat and narrow and capable of slicing off a human head in a single swipe, all mounted upon a huge body with yet another head and four legs, a beast that made a thunderous sound when it ran.

A second example comes from Melanesia. Toward the end of the Great Depression, rumors emerged in Australia that gold had been discovered only a short distance into the interior of southern New Guinea, then a protectorate of Australia. Hundreds headed north, seeking gold, but also fleeing from the dole lines of the Depression. In 1930, Europeans knew little about the interior of this massive island. Indeed, maps listed much of the interior as "unknown." In a short time the coastal finds were depleted, and most of the single claim miners returned home. Three Australian brothers decided to keep up the search. Accompanied by nearly 100 porters, they made their way inland, often scaling mountains ten to twelve thousand feet high. After months on foot they arrived in the Mount Hagen region—almost the center of New Guinea—where no European had been before. The travelers had expected to find no human beings but soon learned that the mountains were home to nearly a million people, who were certain *they* were the only human beings on the earth. The local presumptions were that all people had dark skin, that all men covered their penises with a woven sheath and decorated their nostrils with pig tusks. Unable to recognize these three strange creatures with white faces, almost no skin or visible body parts, local people reasoned that they must be the ghosts of the deceased, now returning to visit them. In terms of indigenous knowledge, this was the only way to make sense of them.

The third example is provided by a record of African exploration, the Roman writer Pliny's popular work titled *Summary of the Antiquities and Wonders of the World*, published in 1556 (cited in Reader, 1998: 325–326):

> Of the Ethiopians there are diverse kinds of men. Some there are toward the east that have neither nose nor nostrils, but the face all full. Others have no upper lip, they are without tongues, and they speak by signs, and they have but a little hole to take their breath at, by which they drink with an oaten straw. There are some called

Syrbote that are eight foot high, and they live with the chase of elephants. In a part of Affricke be people called Ptoemphane, for their
king they have a dog, at whose fancy they are ruled. . . . Toward the
west there are a people called Arimaspi, that hath but one eye on
their foreheads, they are in the desert and the wild country. The people called Agriphagi live with the flesh of panthers and lions: and the
people called Anthropomphagi which we call cannibals, live with human flesh. . . . Blemmyis a people so called, they have no heads but
have their mouth and their eyes in their breasts. And others there
are that walk more by training of their hands than with their feet.

Making sense of the body requires a schema that can be imposed
on the observable world. Such cultural recipes draw attention to some
features and at the same time minimize others. Body sense, or body
perception, thereby consists in part as a process of selective attention.
For men in the highlands of New Guinea natural body adornment con-
sisted of facial cosmetics, bird plumes for the hair, a pig tusk through
the nose and a penis sheath. The "living dead" as they imagine them to
be, had few if any of these features. Apart from a face, the white people
apparently had no body, no genitals, and no way to pass human waste.
Having never seen such creatures, the indigenous people of Mexico may
have wondered if what they saw were previously unknown animals
from the sea. The fanciful woodcut likewise presumes that the human
form is the same in all times and places, as did Pliny in his musings.

THE FACE OF CULTURE

In most human societies the face is the focal point of public interaction. Exceptions to this generalization prove the general rule. In
many Muslim societies, men dominate public life. The exposed female
face is a sign of intimacy, and a woman should expose her face only in
private, domestic company. Veiling the face in public thus becomes a
means to deny symbolically women's public presence. Other habits of
hiding the face—with elaborate masks, with veils, or with hooded capes
in the case of the Ku Klux Klan—are purposefully intended to transform or deny the identity of the person (see Lévi-Strauss, 1982). Para-
doxically, though we regard our faces as distinctly personal possessions, they are the most public part of our bodies. In this light, it is not
a surprise that facial cosmetics and transformation are practices commonly reported from diverse societies.

In many societies of sub-Saharan Africa, facial scarification was a
common means of marking ethnic affiliation and, at the same time, an
expression of particular styles of body aesthetics. Among the Nilotic peoples of the southern Sudan the forehead was the primary focus of facial
adornment. Among the Shilluk young boys and girls pass through a cere-

mony in which a series of pearl-sized lacerations are inscribed across the forehead, running from ear to ear just above the eyebrows. A small fishing hook is pried beneath the skin, which is then severed by a sharp knife. Among the neighboring Dinka, Nuer, and Atuot, distinctive patterns of forehead scarification provide young men public expression of their ethnic affiliation, a matter that was of great significance at an earlier time, when interethnic feuding and cattle raiding were common. Wodaabe men of northern Niger periodically paint their faces in elaborate colorful patterns and are then judged as more or less beautiful by their female suitors, who adorn their faces with permanent tattoos, which not only enhance their beauty but also protect them from the evil eye. The facial decorations of the Bumi of Ethiopia closely resemble those of the Shilluk, but here the scars cross the forehead and also circle the eyes. Among the Tabwa of the Congo, women have deep parallel scars inscribed into their cheeks, which serve as a public mark of their fertility. Elsewhere in Africa, the enlargement of women's lower lips and the elongation of ear lobes express local aesthetics of the body and serve as signs of ethnic identity.

Throughout Polynesia, facial and body tattoos serve as a means of ethnic identification and also function to declare social rank and relative status (see Becker, 1995; Gell, 1993; Hewitt, 1997; Linnekin and Poyer, 1990; Sanders, 1989; Thevoz, 1984). It is interesting to note that early European travelers in this part of the world initially mistook these forms of skin decoration to be elaborate and fine clothing. Among the best described forms of facial tattooing are those for the Maori of New Zealand. Permanent facial tattoos were replicas of Maori ceremonial art, so that an individual's face served as a representation of ancient ceremonial and ancestral belief and behavior—a powerful example of the way in which the "private skin" was a public canvas.

Facial tattooing and painting were also common practices among the diverse cultures in native North America. Europeans coined the pejorative term "red skin" in consequence of these customs. Face painting and tattooing were not only symbols of cultural identity but were also important elements of ritual and ceremonial behavior. In the context of intertribal feuding, masking the skin was a powerful means of empowering the self, a notion common to our own culture. Diverse peoples of Amazonia also employed facial tattooing and painting. Among the Shapibo, for example, the decorative designs painted on pottery were identical to facial tattoos.

In the ethnographic cases cited (and these represent but a smattering of thousands of cultural styles of body transformation) the common theme is the etching of a cultural aesthetic onto the body. Painting the skin creates a temporary second skin, an appropriate technique for ceremonial occasions. In contrast, facial scarification is a permanent transformation of the body. The Western practice of facial and cosmetic surgery is likewise a matter of ethnic and cultural conformity.

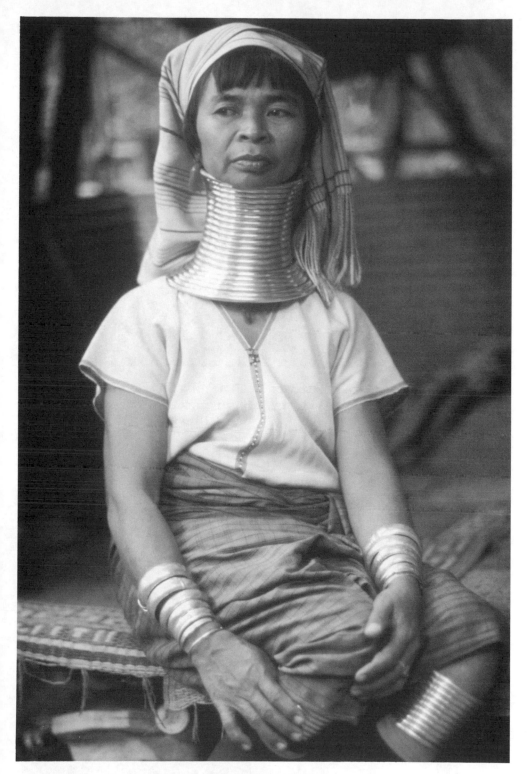

Thai woman wearing neck extension rings.

Disfigured feet of a Chinese woman. The custom of bandaging feet of women of the aristocracy from infancy was still practiced around 1900. Undated photo. (Corbis-Bettmann)

Woman's tattooed leg.

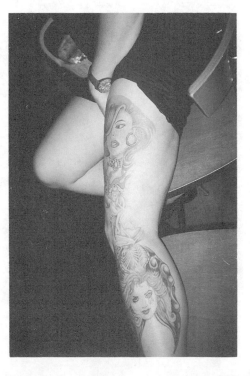

A Toradja priestess in Indonesia ready for her witchcraft.
(Copyright Underwood & Underwood/Corbis)

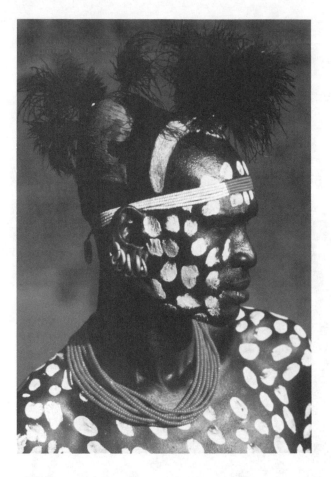

Elaborate hair design, body painting, and multiple piercings of the ear are the trademark of many Karo men in Ethiopia. However, scarification of the chest or wearing a gray and ochre-colored hair bun as the man in this photo does, is allowed only to those who have killed an enemy or a dangerous animal. The same holds true among the Karo's neighbors, the Hamar.
(Copyright Carol Beckwith/Angela Fisher)

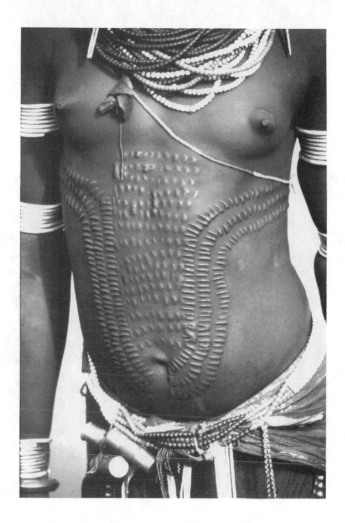

Among the Karo of Ethiopia, the welts raised by body scarification not only are regarded as visual enhancement of beauty,
but also are valued for their tactile erotic quality.
(Copyright Carol Beckwith/Angela Fisher)

Two women in conversation wearing headdresses of wild cat fur with and without their lip plates. It takes only six months to stretch the lips to dimensions that can hold the huge lip-plates of wood or clay that are worn by Suri women in Ethiopia. The plates can easily be taken out for private meals or sleep; otherwise, they may be taken out only when the wearer is in the company of other women. (Copyright Carol Beckwith/Angela Fisher)

MANUFACTURED BODIES

There are a handful of references to permanent facial surgeries in ancient times (see, e.g., Haiken, 1997: 4–5), but in the main cosmetic surgery is a twentieth-century invention. What is now called plastic surgery sometimes has utilitarian value, following trauma, for example, but is also commonly sought as a means to attempt to transform the body to mirror a cultural ideal.

The Western body was once regarded as a divinely constructed phenomenon. Transforming or attempting to control the body was thus regarded as a matter of crude vanity. This ideology persists in the beliefs of Christian Scientists, who regard any manipulation of the body as a form of heresy. However, as North American societies were transformed from rural agrarian modes of existence into urban, consumer-oriented worlds, values about the body and the self were likewise transformed. As Haiken (1997: 7) argues, there emerged from this process an ethos of acquisitive individualism that encouraged us to rethink our body schema. Cosmetic surgery emerged amidst this ideological transformation. "Cosmetic surgery lies at the nexus of medicine and consumer culture. It was the combination of medical knowledge, leisure and money that made possible its entrance on the American stage in the early years of this century" (12).

More precisely, facial and other forms of cosmetic surgery have their roots in the gruesome consequences of World War I. Soldiers suffered physical deformities and disabilities that had never been witnessed or experienced before. While the practice of plastic surgery emerged in the context of medical emergency and crisis, it is now the fastest growing specialization in North American medical technique. According to Haiken (1997: 4) approximately 95 percent of patients are women, propelling an industry that generates some 20 billion dollars per year. In addition to facial alteration, procedures include breast enhancement or reduction, liposuction on the arms, the thighs and the buttocks. Sexual organs are enhanced by both sexes with labia size decreased and penis size increased (Adams, 1997: 66; see also Synott, 1993: 75). Whatever their personal motivation, women and men who decide to have their bodies altered in this way are collectively expressing conformity to an ideal body aesthetic. Cosmetic surgery allows those who think they deviate from others to blend in or stand out, as more than plain, average, or ordinary. In North America, cosmetic culture is an enormous growth industry. The number of fingernail salons, tanning salons, full body waxing salons, and health spas increases daily.

Other well-known practices of social conformity via body alteration include the artificial elongation of the neck in Southeast Asia,

cranial deformation, extreme obesity (as with Japanese sumo wres-
tlers), as well as the former Chinese practice of foot binding (discussed
below). The underlying similarity of these diverse customs of perma
nent body transformation is that they all change an individual's status
and power. Like the cuisine of many cultures, the more highly elaborated the body becomes, the greater social value and esteem it generates. From the perspective of structural anthropology, one can argue
that the more the body is removed from its "natural" state, the more it
is under cultural control and thus more compelling as a symbol of ethnic and cultural identity.

The human foot seems to have an odd appeal to the imagination.
Removing shoes before entering sacred spaces is a common require-
ment in many religious traditions. In many Muslim societies, in northern India and in Southeast Asia, women often spend hours painting
designs on their feet with henna dye or drape their ankles and toes
with silver or gold chains. High fashion in the West often demands that
women wear shoes with extremely high heels, which make walking
both difficult and dangerous.

The most elaborated "pediculture" known in human history was the
Chinese tradition of foot binding (see Farizza, 1996; Jackson, 1997; Levy,
1966). According to Levy (1966: 17), this practice was initially developed
by dancers whose performances were staged for political elites: "Court
circles and the upper class at large imitated the fashion, and soon it
became a status symbol." Typically a woman's foot was allowed to grow
no more than three or four inches long, and contests were held to award
women with the tiniest feet. In this condition, an adult woman was
unable to walk without assistance. Possessing tiny bound feet was thus
a symbol of high status, since only the well-to-do could afford a full-time
handmaiden to assist in the task. There was an erotic dimension to the
practice as well. According to Farazza (1996: 139):

> The ecstasy experienced by Chinese men upon seeing or fondling a
> lotus foot was the equivalent of that experienced by western men
> upon seeing or fondling a female breast. The Chinese also believed,
> however, that foot-binding had a special bonus, namely, it caused
> layer after layer of folds to develop in the vagina, resulting in a su-
> pernatural exaltation during intercourse. The inability to walk
> supposedly also caused the woman's thighs to become sensually
> heavier and caused the genital region to tighten.

One older woman recalled:

> "I remember that when the binding first began, I did not feel pain
> and, in fact, thought it very interesting. My mother told me that only
> through foot-binding could a woman become more beautiful. . . . My
> mother did not feel bad when she saw me in pain because she was
> doing this to enhance my attractiveness. My feet, even after ten

years of age, did not feel pain, but only restricted. Perhaps other
girls secretly removed their bandages, but if their mothers found
out, they were either beaten or the binding was sewn to prevent its
being loosened." (quoted in Levy, 1966: 250)

Another woman observed:

There was also a practical factor involved in the degree to which
feet were reduced, for while a mother wished that her daughter's
feet be as small as possible, she had to consider the economic situation of the family. If the family expected the girl to work in the future, her feet could not be too small. So, many women did not bind
their feet. (Levy, 1996:1 251).

IDENTITY ON THE SKIN

The modern nation-state has greater knowledge about and control over our minds and bodies than at any other point in human history. As Shilling (1993: 2) writes, our condition of modernity "has facil-
itated an increase in Western societies of the degree of control that the
nation-state in general, and the medical profession in particular, have
been able to exert over the bodies of their citizens." Increasingly in
Western societies, grand narratives of religious and political truths are
abandoned. A growing number of parents have decided to home-school
their children. Alternative forms of religious practice are more common. Fewer people than ever participate in national elections. Concurrently, capitalistic culture has vastly multiplied products to satisfy our
particular and individual cravings, particularly regarding body culture. Giddens (1991: 7) observes, "What might appear as a wholesale
movement towards the narcissistic cultivation of body appearance is in
fact an expression of a concern lying much deeper."

What lies much deeper? As members of Western societies are ever
more constrained by external, impersonal forms of social control, the
body has become the singular focus of self-control and identity. Personal ownership of the body is the order of the day; yet, as in the case
of cosmetic surgery, people are attending to the cultivation of the individual body in droves. Current fashions of body transformation, such as
piercing and tattooing, have come to be known collectively as "modern
primitivism," an oxymoron if ever there was one. Modern primitivism
has emerged as a feature of popular culture in association with
renewed concerns about environmental issues as well as a sentimental
fascination with so-called "primitive" peoples.

Older stereotypes of people who transformed their skin include
pirates, criminals, and other social deviants. Those who were secluded
from wider society often inscribed their bodies with centrally signifi-

cant social symbols: images of mothers, Valentine-shaped hearts, and religious icons, reminders of life that could not be experienced in a prison cell or a three-year long whaling voyage.

In North America and Europe, the increasing popularity of piercing and tattooing indicates that these forms of body decoration are in fact becoming a part of mainstream culture (see, e.g., Barker and Tietjen, 1990; Bell, 1949; Bohannan, 1956; Camphausen, 1997; Demello, 1993; Rosenblatt, 1997; Rubin, 1988; Tannenbaum, 1987). Hundreds of Web sites advertise products, techniques, and styles. While tattoos are an intimate expression of personal aesthetics, they are simultaneously a mark of collective identity and belonging. Tattoo and piercing conventions bring together thousands of people from diverse backgrounds, who all share a common form of body language. Sanders (1988: 230) writes, "Tattooees conceive of the tattoo as having an impact on their definition of self and demonstrating to others information about their unique interests and social connections." As a professional practitioner of the craft he speaks with some authority and has in fact created a "typology of motivations" for those who choose to be tattooed. The first of these are individuals who are motivated to use their skin as a symbol of interpersonal relationships. Someone will choose a particular tattoo because it resembles that of a close friend or family member. Group association is Sanders's second category. For example, military personnel select tattoos that indicate their service connection and specialization, motorcycle club members choose a common insignia, and participants in religious sects opt for appropriate icons of their beliefs. Sanders denotes a third category as motivation for self-identity, which may have magical qualities. As one of his clients related:

> I'm allergic to bees. If I get stung again I'm going to die. So I thought I'd come in and have a big mean-looking bee put on. I want one that has this long stinger and these long teeth and is coming in to land. With that, any bee would think twice about messing with me. (1988: 222)

Finally, there are those who have tattoos purely for the purpose of a decorative or aesthetic experience. On occasion, these are individuals who want to cover a perceived body imperfection, such as a birthmark or tissue scar.

The growing literature on this practice suggests there is a gendered aspect of tattooing. Men generally have larger and bolder tattoos with stereotypically masculine symbols, while women tend to choose flowers or butterflies. In either case, tattoos range from covering the full body to a single location, on the breast, the arm, the back, the ankle or the genital region.

North American societies normally demand that the body be modestly covered in public settings. Tattoos thus represent a liminal dialogue between public and private life. For all you know, your medical doctor, mortgage officer, or minister may be covered with tattoos, but as long as conventional clothing hides the skin, one will never know. The same applies to techniques of body piercing.

Body piercing in European and North American societies was initially popularized as an emblem of "punk" culture, as an overt means of social protest. Yet by now body-piercing venues have become as common as fast-food restaurants. No single fact can account for the growing popularity of this practice, which instead invites a number of different interpretive perspectives.

From the perspective of many non-Western societies, the Euro-American attempt to remain forever young must appear odd in the extreme. In these social worlds, the younger generation is forced to learn and embody customs that are dictated by their elders. Tradition isn't questioned; it is enforced. In Western societies, by contrast, each generation takes it upon itself to question, protest, or otherwise contest established norms. The practice of body piercing has been interpreted as one such form of protest: this is my body, and I will do with it as I please. Placing pieces of metal through the nose, tongue, ear, navel, nipple, or genitals was not something an earlier generation did and is therefore something "I" will do. As one of my daughter's friends recently said, "I just turned eighteen, so there is no way my parents can stop me from having my tongue pierced." Although perceived as an expression of individual choice, her decision to do this was in fact an unconscious effort to conform to collective contemporary fashion, to adopt a counterculture identity.

Yet, as a growing number of adults adopt the practice, body piercing can no longer be regarded as a symbolic expression of protest and individualism. The social skin can also be regarded as a medium of collective discourse. Gender equality has been a collective ideal over the past thirty years: that both women and men can do similar things to their own bodies reflects this fact, as does the emergence of unisex hair salons and the pedestrian attire commonly selected by women and men: jeans, sneakers and a T-shirt.

Still another plausible motivation for the body-piercing fashion is an attempt to increase emotive power. The use of penile inserts (see Brown, Edwards, and Moore, 1988) in Southeast Asia has been interpreted as a custom that had both aesthetic and erotic appeal. Some women who have had nipple, clitoral, or labial piercings report that this heightens sexual arousal and response. Practitioners suggest that these types of body alteration are more common than might initially be expected (see, e.g., Camphausen, 1997: 75–79).

The phrase *modern primitivism* invites further commentary. Many of those who participate in the practice of body piercing identify themselves as "tribals" and do as they do in emulation of so-called "tribal" or "primitive" peoples. In fact, these contemporary customs are neither tribal nor primitive. The term *tribal* is a technical, anthropological term that refers to a particular form of political organization, and there hasn't been a primitive society around for the past million years. Rather, the phrase reflects a romantic Western fabrication of some distant and "other" people, who live in an imaginary harmony with their bodies and their environment. This collective misrepresentation has a long history in Western thought and originated in the philosophical musings of authors during the so-called age of discovery. Certainly there is nothing "primitive" about transforming the body: this is an element of every human society, past and present. The phrase connotes instead a hint of identification with the victims of Western development and destruction (see Rosenblatt, 1997: 302). Through the manipulation of their bodies, modern primitives seek to establish an identity with a mythical image of a more pristine and authentic existence (Rosenblatt, 1997: 318).

A number of ironies emerge from this attempt to emulate a mythical primitive world through body modification. Often, as in Amazonian cultures, body decorations are temporary: paint adorns the body only on ceremonial occasions. Permanent body scarification is hardly a universal in the mythical primitive world imagined by modern primitives. Romantic nostalgia aside, who among the self-proclaimed modern primitives would really want to abandon electricity, private transportation, and a vast array of material comforts to live in a rain forest with choking humidity, dangerous and bothersome insects, and poisonous snakes, so that they could kill monkeys with a blowgun for dinner? It is more likely that their self-chosen means of body adornment is a symbol of disaffection with contemporary culture rather than a sincere effort to emulate a life they will never know. In any case, transforming the body in this way is best regarded as a means of achieving a novel form of collective identity, even while it is perceived as a means of self-conscious and individual expression.

TEMPORARY SKIN

Powerful statements about society and the individual are also made through the manipulation of the temporary skin we call clothing. What we in the West regard as normal ways to adorn and hide the body are in fact fairly recent products of industrialism and mass manufacture (see, e.g., Barthes, 1983; Bergler, 1953; Coleridge, 1988; Hollander, 1980; Joseph, 1986; Kaiser, 1985; Lauer and Lauer, 1981; Lurie, 1981; O'Hara, 1986; Polhemus and Proctor, 1978; Weiner and Schneider, 1989). Well into the last century, indigenous peoples manufactured clothing from local plant and animal resources. The cultural attention given to exposing or hiding body parts varies considerably and seems to change in relation to local notions of modesty and eroticism. Ecological factors have surely had an influence on local practice. The "naked savages" encountered by Europeans of northern latitudes were not naked at all, but rather adorned in a manner suitable to their habitats and customs. Europeans interpreted exposed breasts and other body parts as evidence of promiscuous sexuality. (This is evidence of a fundamental misunderstanding, much like the assertion that native men of New England were lazy and idle folk since they spent their time fishing and hunting. From the European perspective, these were pursuits of sports enthusiasts; from the native point of view, such activities were fundamental to survival!) In all human societies fundamentally important matters such as gender, social status, rank, and age are marked by body adornment and forms of clothing.

Davis (1992: 13) makes the incontestable observation that the meaning of body costume is culturally specific. Clothing style is the signature costume of culture. Anthropologist Christopher Steiner (1990) has developed this point in an ingenious manner that suggests a correlation between styles of temporary body adornment and systems of political authority and control. He points out that in many Melanesian societies, political authority traditionally rested in the hands of "big men"—individuals who, by their charisma and patronage, wielded positions of public authority in social worlds that were not founded on bureaucratic process and norms. Big men were not elected officials; nor was this status inherited across generations. Rather, a big man's authority derived purely from his personal presence and persona. His power was temporary, open to the challenge of any and all others who would seek to claim similar status. His public body, Steiner argues, carried with it equally temporal and transient symbols of authority: a painted face, bird plumes, and other readily removable decorations. Steiner suggests that the big man's symbols of power were as easily removed as the authority they were meant to represent.

In Polynesian societies, by contrast, indigenous polities were rigidly stratified and were founded upon principles of inherited rank and status across generations. Chiefly classes were distinguished from commoner classes by the tattoos of rank that were permanently inscribed on their bodies. As Steiner (1990: 432) writes:

> While Polynesian societies are typified by fixed hierarchy and minuscule amounts of social mobility, Melanesian societies are characterized by a more fluid social structure with a great deal of individual mobility and change in status. In the former system, both groups and individuals are related to one another in permanent dyadic relations of superior to inferior; in the latter system, the power of status differential between both groups and individuals continually shifts.

Thus the notable difference in the second skin: in Melanesia, any man may someday don the feathers and the painted face of fleeting political authority; in Polynesia the royalty of political authority carried with it permanent forms of body transformation.

In this chapter attention has been drawn to a wide variety of cultural contexts and ethnographic facts relating to the ways in which cultural identity is inscribed on the human body, from names to faces, surgery, and clothing. To know who we are, both as individuals and as members of groups with whom we identify, we also have to know who we are not. Much of this is a silent dialogue, carried out between the individual body and the social world in which it lives. Anthropologists would assert that much of this information is processed and internalized unconsciously. But the body is also used as a conscious template to delineate who we want other people to think we are, and therefore whom we want to be identified with. We find who we are in a process of finding out who we are not. As Steiner (1990) intimates, this entails a political dimension of all human experience in every human society.

Chapter Four

Him and Her
Initiation and the Body

Arnold Van Gennep was a close colleague of Durkheim. Although Van Gennep never carried out ethnographic fieldwork, his major life's work focused on the comparative study of ethnographic information. Much of the information available to him had been collected by untrained and sometimes biased observers, but he was certain that one could observe general laws about social behavior in the positivistic tradition of Durkheim. In 1909 Van Gennep (1960) published his landmark monograph *The Rites of Passage,* a broadly comparative study of initiation and life crisis rituals. He observed that in most human societies significant transitions in the life cycle are publicly recognized and culturally "controlled" by ritual activity. He demonstrated that while the cultural content of these rituals varied enormously, rites of passage always appeared to be structures in an identical form. There is a period of separation from quotidian life, a time of status transformation and a final occasion of reincorporation into secular society. Van Gennep's general interest was not in the details of particular rituals or ceremonial occasions, but with discerning their underlying, systematic form. That initiation rituals take such consistent form throughout diverse human societies suggests there are universal similarities in the human imagination as well as systems of symbolic classification (see, e.g., Needham, 1973).

Van Gennep was particularly interested in rituals that are enacted in situations of individual or social crisis, such as pregnancy and birth, the transition from adolescent to adult status, and rituals performed in the situation of death. He was careful to emphasize that ritual activity is a regular component of almost every social convention. While we are rarely conscious of the fact, our daily lives are embedded in and constrained by personal and collective ritual behavior. However, in *The*

Rites of Passage, Van Gennep was primarily interested in various rituals that serve to transform an individual's social status.

IIis insights are relevant here since it can be argued that initiation rituals are the most important social occasion of marking and defining a culturally constructed concept of gender and gender differentiation. Stated in slightly different terms, initiation rituals define how women are different from men and how men are different from women. From the anthropological perspective, they provide a key symbol of how the natural fact of sexual difference is embedded with cultural meaning. The anthropological literature on this topic is vast. Here I focus on a small number of specific ethnographic cases: the Sambia of highland New Guinea, the Wogeo of Melanesia, the Tiv of Nigeria and the Kaguru of Tanzania. These societies do not provide an ideal basis for cross-cultural comparison. The peoples named have distinctive cultural traditions, practice different modes of livelihood, and also differ in terms of scale and social complexity. They are chosen for discussion because gifted anthropologists have described them with enviable skill. Prior to this review, it is worthwhile to consider a number of anthropological perspectives on initiation ritual in general.

RITUAL AND STATUS

The *Oxford English Dictionary* provides a number of entries under the term *initiate*, including to begin, to set going, to admit. Each of these notions has significance for a full understanding of initiation ritual. In its popular usage the phrase *initiation ritual* connotes practices of peoples distant from North American society perhaps and images of tribal people singing, grunting, and dancing. However, there are numerous occasions in our own lives when changes in status are marked by symbolic practices: becoming a Girl Scout, joining a fraternity, becoming a partner in a legal firm, or being inaugurated into a role of political prominence. If there is a general contrast between "modern" and "traditional" societies in this regard, it is that "we" as women and men" have no singular and common form of gender initiation.

From a comparative perspective, initiation rituals share a number of common themes. Often, they are overtly focused on the domestication of sexuality and the redefinition of social status that this entails. In this sense, they can be regarded as a cultural (that is, artificial) attempt to control and give meaning to the natural process of aging and maturity. They mark the passage of time. Van Gennep (1960 [1909]: 71) emphasized that initiation ceremonies are not necessarily puberty ceremonies. Rather, they mark the end of childhood, which may or may not correspond with physical and sexual maturity. He made this argument in regard to the practice of clitoridectomy, which may occur several weeks after birth, when a girl is four years old, or when she is an adolescent. In a parallel way, he pointed out, male circumcision can take place moments after birth or well into adolescence. Van Gennep stressed that initiation ceremonies are socially constructed occasions that serve to mark changes in social status; they may or may not correspond to biological phenomena.

As a consequence, new social relationships are created and expressed through initiation. For example, in many cultures, young boys and girls grow up in socially identical worlds. Initiation rituals frequently serve as a means to emphasize what is properly feminine behavior, and what is properly masculine behavior. Initiation rituals are also occasions which redefine legitimacy by reaffirming systems of hierarchy and authority. Often, in order to be recognized as an adult, and thus gain access to adult knowledge, young children must endure a physical or emotional ordeal. The aboriginal Australian custom of the "walkabout" is an apt illustration. Here, young men were forced to live in solitude in the arid wilderness, often for an extended period of time—as Van Gennep would stress, separated from society in every way imaginable. In numerous Plains Indian cultures of North America, young men undertook a similar form of vision quest. Upon his reentry into social life, elders questioned the young man about his emotional and spiritual journey. If his experiences were deemed to be authentic by village elders, his attainment of adult status was celebrated. In many Western societies state-enforced military training provides a closely analogous example for postadolescent women and men. In these ways, tradition is recreated and conformity is enforced.

Another common feature of initiation ceremonies entails a theme of symbolic death and rebirth—the erasure of one social status and social personality and the creation of a new identity. Betwixt and between these status changes is a period that Van Gennep termed the liminal state, a term derived from the Latin *limen*, or threshold. Until the status transition is completed, the initiate is both part of the past and not quite part of the future. It is a period in which the normal cosmological order may be inverted or denied. The North American custom of a New Year's Eve party provides an apt illustration: during the liminal period between the old year and the new, people often engage in behaviors that might be unthinkable under normal circumstances.

Initiation ceremonies of one sort or another are nearly universal in human social life. Why this might be so is a question that has garnered considerable academic attention. Social existence is possible only when individuals conform to normative patterns of behavior. Nature is everywhere under the influence of cultural formulas. Human beings seek to order the universe around them. Imposing hierarchy is one such instance. Most primate species live within hierarchies based upon sex and age: dominant males oversee the behavior of their temporal juniors. Human initiation ceremonies have a similar consequence. Our animate existence is only masked by culture. Creating and maintaining age and dominance hierarchies is one of the most common themes of initiation ceremonies.

Brain (1977) has argued that initiation rituals for adolescent females serve as a public means to announce the metamorphosis of their lives from asexual into sexual beings. Since it is women, rather than men, who organize female initiation ceremonies, Brain argues that these occasions provide a means for older women to assert and maintain their authority over their daughters. Initiation ceremonies for young girls are commonly the occasion when mothers instruct their daughters about adult femininity and sexuality. Conversely, he suggests, male initiation ceremonies are intended to control the younger generation through either painful or psychologically threatening behavior. Brown (1963; see also Driver, 1969; Rigby, 1967; Young, 1965) has sought to explain why female initiation ceremonies are found in some, but not all, human societies. She has also tried to explain why these rituals differ in form and content. She suggests that female initiation rites primarily occur in societies where females continue to live in their natal villages after marriage, that is, where there is a postmarital rule of matrilocal residence. Concurrently, she suggests, in those societies where women's subsistence activities are very important, rituals of female initiation are most likely to occur. Young (1965: 1) argues rituals of status transition such as initiation vary in association with the degree of social solidarity and social control. These latter approaches to the basic question are best regarded as extreme examples of sociological determinism.

Bettelheim (1968 [1954]) on the other hand, is well known for his more psychological and Freudian-inspired interpretation of initiation and body transformation. There is no way to construct an original scenario that gave rise to customs of initiation. Bettelheim (1968 [1954]: 15) suggests, however, that since these ritual forms are so common across a diverse range of human societies, they express a "deep human need." From this perspective, male circumcision is a symbolic substitute for castration, "a punishment which the primevial father dealt his sons out of the fullness of his power; and whoever accepted this symbol showed by doing so that he was ready to submit to the father's will, although it was at the cost of painful sacrifice." In Bettelheim's view, forms of male initiation that entail some form of genital transformation manifest a male desire or fantasy to be female. As he argues (45), "One purpose of male initiation rites may be to assert that men, too, can bear children. . . . Through subincision men try to acquire sexual apparatus and functions equivalent to women's." Stated in symbolic rather than psychoanalytic terms, Bettelheim's argument suggests that forms of male initiation are a cultural effort to mimic and thereby control what appears to be a "naturally" feminine capability—to produce children (see also Rosaldo and Lamphere, 1974).

Shilling (1993: 108; see also Brain, 1988; Caplan, 1980; LaFontaine, 1985; Lang, 1998; Ramet, 1996; Walker and Parmar, 1993) sees the issue from an entirely different perspective and argues that initiation rituals are intended to emphasize biological differences between women and men:

> The suppression of body similarities is most obvious in the case of young children who have gender identities imposed on them long before they are capable of reproducing. . . . Similarities between their bodies are neglected, differences are fabricated, or exaggerated, and the meanings of biological features are changed into new sets of categories and oppositions.

From this perspective, in other words, the cultural elaboration of sexual differences is one of the primary functions of initiation rituals.

In an equally fundamental way, initiation rituals are a play on opposites: one is a member of this group, one is not a member; one is either an insider or an outsider; one is truly a woman or one is truly a man. To some, this play on opposites is a cultural elaboration of human biology. The anthropologist T. O. Beidelman (1980: 144) has argued "despite the fact that particular sexual roles are greatly determined by culture rather than by nature, important differences occur which suggest that at certain levels *women are more deeply beings of their biology than men*" (emphasis added). In other words, the suggestion here is that the roles of men are more subject to cultural elaboration than are those of women. From this perspective, male sexuality and masculine status are dependent upon a conceptual scheme, while female sexuality is more or less given. Beidelman (1980: 162) writes, "it must be of some significance that men must be sexually aroused to father children, whereas women may conceive frigidly." In fact, this is a suspect observation, and one that is physiologically inaccurate. Female orgasm greatly increases the chance of conception, since during orgasm, the cervix opens and dips down in order to accept sperm.

As suggested earlier, the interpretation and understanding of ethnographic information is best sought from a number of different theoretical perspectives. In reference to initiation and the transformation of the body, sociological, psychological, and biological factors are all significant. With that noted, these differing theoretical perspectives may be assessed in regard to a number of ethnographic case studies.

THE SAMBIAN WORLD

As far as we can be certain, the interior highlands of Papua New Guinea were first inhabited by human beings beginning some 50,000 years before the present, during a period of geologic history when land bridges connected islands and continents now separated by oceans and seas. Reasoned speculation suggests that the first human beings who lived in New Guinea subsisted by hunting and gathering, as did all of humanity 10,000 years before the present. Domesticated pigs were eventually introduced into this region, and in the course of time, yam cultivation and pig rearing became the backbone of local life. At the time of European contact, New Guinea was home to some 700 distinct human languages. Adapting to an extreme diversity of environmental zones, from coastal plains and mangrove swamps to steep slopes on interior mountains, New Guinea became home to diverse human cultures. In the highlands, local societies were fairly small in number and fluid in terms of social organization. The center of political life was a big man, an individual who by his charisma and personal style mediated and directed village life. His authority was circumstantial and was often a matter of his success or failure in leading raids against local villages— to capture women and to avenge similar raids against his own village.

At the time of European contact, intervillage raiding was endemic and formed the basis of local political organization. People fought to assure that they held claim to sufficient land for gardening and pig rearing. In most highland societies, adult men gained status and prestige in association with their bravado and success in warfare.

Among the Sambia, as in numerous other highland societies, there exists an extreme form of sexual antagonism and a rigid division of labor between women and men. It is as though they live in separate worlds. Men fell trees to clear garden plots; cultivation is primarily a woman's effort. Men hunt, but women are prohibited from this. While women and children tend pig herds, men own the animals. Even the staple crops are gendered. Since yams and sweet potatoes are soft and grown in the ground horizontally, they are regarded as feminine. Taro, on the other hand, is hard and grows vertically and is thus considered to be masculine.

The physical setting of village life is also bounded by gendered space. In hamlets, men build large long houses that can only be visited by males: women are threatened with rape or murder should they enter this space. During her period, a woman resides in a menstrual hut some distance away from her own home and on the periphery of the hamlet. This is also where she goes to give birth. Sambian men view menstruation and childbirth as highly "polluting" phenomena and so insist that at these times, women must be removed from quotidian life so that masculine power will not be compromised. Inside the domestic hut, physical space is also marked by powerful taboos. A wife and her children occupy one side of the hut while the other side is entirely the domain of the husband. Women are forbidden to enter the husband's side of the hut lest their physical presence compromise his masculinity. Men cross the women's space as a matter of course to enter their own "sacred" space.

In the past, while women toiled in the gardens, took care of children, and fed the pigs, men contemplated when and where the next intertribal feud would be staged. As Herdt (1987: 25) writes, Sambian men were "preoccupied" with warfare. With their father's attention always focused on the possibility of violent confrontations, young children could find stability and security only in their mother's presence. Schwartz (1973: 157) has drawn attention to the modal personality that emerged:

> The paranoid ethos in Melanesia derived from uncertainty of life, from the high mortality rate and short life span, from many who died in childbirth, and few surviving children. It depended on the uncertainty of the yield of productive activities. Perhaps more fundamentally for Melanesia, the paranoid ethos related to the extreme atomism of social and political life, to the constancy of war and raiding.

Since warfare and the protection of village territory were entirely adult male endeavors, women and children were denied general knowledge about the secret world of men. As in ancient Greece, warfare and male secrecy were cornerstones of Sambian society. (In both cases, there are reasons to surmise that women encouraged this aura of ignorance.)

From the local perspective, the essence of masculinity is termed *jerungdu*, a term Herdt (1987: 31) translates as "male strength" and its associated qualities, such as physical strength, strength in warfare, and strength to defend oneself and property. Women and small children lack this quality since jerungdu is the essential quality of semen. In the Sambian view, during gestation, it is semen that creates the "hard" parts of the body. Herdt (1987: 31) notes that Sambian men believe that the masculine life force hinges on possessing abundant jerungdu. Sambian men claim that this power is constantly threatened by women, particularly as a consequence of intercourse. As one man lamented (34) "No wonder women are healthy and outlive us." Women are thought to grow stronger through the incorporation of semen.

In consequence of these ideas, there emerges a fundamental dilemma for Sambian men: to be a real adult, a man must be a successful warrior. He must also be the father of a large family. Both activities are a continual drain of his jerungdu. As much as men seek to gain fame as warriors and successful husbands, they also live in perpetual fear of contagion from women. Herdt (1987: 41) puts the matter in these terms:

> The state of maleness is not the gift of nature. Masculinity, in all respects, is a personal achievement. The ethic of *jerungdu*, instilled throughout the long initiations into manhood, compels men to be dominant in all manner of interpersonal relationships and activities, thus ensuring that *jerungdu* is a governing principle of Sambian life.

For the Sambia, adult masculinity is thus a cultural achievement rather than a natural, biological fact. Cultivating this quality is the essential task of adult men through the initiation of young boys. By contrast, Sambian girls are thought to achieve adult sexuality and femininity as a natural process. They are said to possess a self-activating blood organ called *tingu* that begins the process of menstruation and functions naturally throughout a woman's life. Herdt (1987: 76) observes that for young boys, "two obstacles block male growth. The first is their mother's pollution, food, and over-all caretaking, which nurtures them but stifles their growth. The second is their lack of semen, because the semen organ can only store, and not manufacture semen." Men say that when women swallow semen during oral sex, it flows to their breasts and produces milk. By this reasoning, boys must be "fed" semen since they are incapable of producing it themselves.

Before the time that they have shown any sign of secondary sexual development, boys are gathered together by men and taken to live in initiation camps, some distance from their natal hamlets. For a number of days they are taunted and physically abused; they are not allowed sleep for consecutive nights. Next they are taught the practice of blowing long flutes, the first step in mastering the technique of homosexual oral sex. A boy's father selects a guardian for the young initiate, who acts as a tutor and guide throughout the initiation process. For a period of three to five years, the boy will perform oral sex with his guardian. During this extended period boys are repeatedly threatened and psychologically abused. For example, they are told that adult men will cut off their penises if they ever attempt adultery or reveal the secrets of male initiation to females. At the end of the initiation procedures, each sponsor carries his client on his back through a gauntlet some twenty yards long. Two parallel rows of men await them, and as they pass through, whip the boys' backs with sharp bamboo fronds. The boys emerge from this trial bloodied, confused and, most importantly, re-born. Indeed, this closing ceremony can be likened to a reenactment of birth. Here, however, it is men, not women, who symbolically give birth. In Herdt's (1987: 151) terms, the boys have to be killed so that they can be reborn as men.

When these young adults eventually become married men, their first sexual involvement with their wives is primarily oral, because, as previously mentioned, men assert that women must consume semen so that their breasts will fill with milk. A girl's first menstruation is taken as the sign of her sexual maturity, and following this, the married couple engage in heterosexual intercourse. Concurrently, when his wife is menstruating, a man commences the monthly ritual of nose bleeding, an act that removes the "pollution" he experiences from intimate relations. In order to replenish their semen after intercourse, men travel into the surrounding forest and slice the bark of a tree that produces a thick, white sap, which they then swallow. This has the double effect of cleaning them from the pollution of intercourse and also restoring their jerungdu.

Herdt has termed this initiation practice as a form of "ritualized homosexuality." I doubt that this usage would initially make sense to Sambian men. Rather, the ethnographic record for this part of the world suggests that men feel compelled to take "nature" into their own hands, to control it. Masculinity must be culturally imposed upon imperfectly formed, fragile bodies. Sambian femininity is a natural fact and invites no further cultural elaboration. Masculinity, by contrast, is inherently amorphous, always threatened, and can only be realized by controlling nature. For the Sambia, femininity is an ascribed status, while masculinity is an achieved status.

WOMEN AND MEN IN WOGEO

In 1970, the late British anthropologist Ian Hogbin published a monograph with the intriguing title *The Island of Menstruating Men* (rpt. 1996 [1976]). Wogeo is one of the Schouten Islands, located off the northeast coast of Papua New Guinea, some thirty miles off shore from the mouth of the Sepik River. When Hogbin lived here in 1934, it was inhabited by approximately 900 people. The island was occupied temporarily by Japanese armed forces during World War II, but during Hogbin's stay, half a decade earlier than the outbreak of the war, there was little evidence of European or any other foreign influence.

In the 1930s the peoples of Wogeo gained their subsistence through the cultivation of taro and bananas, trapping wild pigs, and fishing from the sea. Every five to six years trading expeditions were mounted to neighboring islands to exchange manufactured goods. Political organization was based on a loose system of headmanships. Social hierarchy was minimal, and most larger-scale corporate activity centered on islandwide systems of prestation and countergift exchange.

According to Hogbin (1996 [1970]: 86), if it were a perfect world on Wogeo, women would live and work by themselves, as would men. From the local perspective, however, women are attracted to men as men are attracted to women, and there are unavoidable consequences. Because of economic and physical interdependence, Hogbin (1996 [1970]: 88) writes that "the entire population is perpetually weakened, liable to disease and misadventure—males because of their association with females, females because of their association with males." In the Wogeo view, women are inherently superior physical beings in comparison to men. Menstruation is regarded as a natural feminine process that habitually purifies women from their contact with men. When a man's son begins to evidence signs of secondary sexual development, he will teach him a technique to scarify and pierce his tongue. The act is intended as a means to cleanse him of the ritual pollution he has amassed from prolonged, prepubescent contact with his mother. The onset of puberty, in other words, is marked on the body as a cultural technique to imitate the natural process of female menstruation. Prolonged intimate relations between spouses are likewise regarded as ritually polluting and dangerous. A woman is freed from this taint through her monthly period. In contrast, adult men are ever in danger of ritual pollution and therefore must cleanse themselves artificially following sexual encounters. They must also menstruate.

Hogbin (1996 [1970]: 88–89) observes:

> First the man catches a crayfish or crab and removes one of the claws, which he keeps wrapped up in ginger until it is required. He also collects various soothing leaves. . . . from dawn onwards on the day he has fixed he eats nothing. Then late in the afternoon he goes to a lonely beach, covers his head with a palm spathe, removes his clothing, and wades out until the water is up to his knees. He stands there with legs apart and induces an erection. . . . When ready, he pushes back the foreskin and hacks at the glans, first on the left side, then on the right. Above all, he must not allow the blood to fall on his fingers or his legs. He waits till the cut is dry and the sea is no longer pink and then walks to shore. After wrapping the penis in leaves, he dresses and goes back to the village.

Throughout his marital career a man will repeat this process—if not on a monthly basis, then at least in accord with any perceived change in his general health. If a common illness fails to respond to customary treatment, the next diagnosis hints at feminine impurities and thus the need to make his penis menstruate again (91). With this ritual remedy completed, Hogbin observes:

> The salutary effects of penile surgery are said to be immediately observable. The man's body loses its tiredness, his muscles harden, his step quickens, his eyes grow bright, and his skin and hair develop a luster. He therefore feels lighthearted, strong and confident. . . . Warriors make sure to menstruate before setting out on a raid, traders before carving an overseas canoe or refurbishing its sails, hunters before weaving new net for trapping pigs. (91)

As among the Sambia, Wogeo men believe that young boys have to be cultivated into true men. As noted, in their youth, boys learn to pierce their tongues to purify them from feminine associations. Following puberty boys move their residence from their mother's home to the village men's house. Soon after, they are instructed how to incise their penises. According to Hogbin (1996 [1970]: 121), when a young man become sexually active, he will join an age-mate or friend in a lagoon and slash his penis with a sharp crab shell, making sure that the gash produces copious amounts of blood. When this procedure is completed, he returns to the men's house and remains secluded until the wound heals. With his masculine identity established, he becomes a "true man," separated in most every way from the women's world and able to free himself from their naturally superior bodies.

KAGURU INITIATION AND MORALITY

According to the anthropologist T. O. Beidelman (1997), among the Kaguru of Tanzania, male and female initiation provides the basis of moral experience. In his view, initiation is simultaneously an expression of deep moral beliefs, gender norms and roles, as well as a public declaration of ethnic distinctiveness and identity. Beidelman suggests that Kaguru initiation is also concerned with two types of identity and transformation. It clearly marks the Kaguru as a separate social and cultural group and transforms the child into an adult. Adults do not consider children to be full social beings. As in every other society, Kaguru children are socialized to accept the world around them as the most natural way to live as a human being. Beidelman's Kaguru informants stressed upon him the belief that initiation rituals were one of the most important components of their culture since they serve to transform children into adults. Beidelman (1997: 2) writes:

> This initiation involves what Durkheim termed moral education, by which humans become aware that they have no meaningful identity outside society. Such initiation transforms 'raw' human beings into social, cultural persons through the beliefs, values, and customs of the society that envelops them.

During Beidelman's first fieldwork in the late 1950s, the Kaguru numbered approximately 100,000. They procured most of their livelihood through horticulture, growing maize, various types of beans, bananas, tobacco, and millet. Kaguru also tended herds of goats and sheep and kept small herds of cattle.

According to Kaguru elders, no matter what his age or biological characteristics, a male would never be socially recognized as an adult until he had undergone the ritual of circumcision. Although initiation may accompany the onset of physical maturity, the two phenomena are not linked in Kaguru thought. Men stressed that the act itself should be painful and that the pain of circumcision should always be remembered. Beidelman (1997: 134) observes:

> The pain and consequent psychic vulnerability generated by this operation should be utilized as a means for transforming information and teaching discipline to the initiate. None of this would succeed if the initiate were not sufficiently old enough to be impressed; it would be lost on a true infant, such as one cut according to Muslim custom.

Preparations for this life-altering ritual are complex, and they entail the teaching of significant ethical and moral practice and belief.

Boys must first be prepared for the ritual. it is an ordeal that they anticipate with dread. A boy's father typically begins the process through consultation with senior kin. It must be agreed collectively that the transition to adulthood is justified. In the course of several acts of divination, ancestors are also addressed, and their approval is sought as further sanction for the event. Male initiation usually takes place during the dry season, when food is plentiful and people are freed from typical subsistence activities. The boy's father must also select a man who has a good reputation as a circumciser as well as knowledge of traditional medicines, used to heal the wound and also ward off witchcraft (Beidelman, 1997: 137). On the perimeter of domestic settlements, a short distance "in the bush," men built an initiation camp, essentially a small shelter with a thatched roof. To the Kaguru, cutting the foreskin is an activity that is symbolically "hot" and therefore ritually dangerous. Once the operation has been completed, the initiates remain under the "cool" protection of the shelter while their wounds heal.

Just before the operation all body hair is shaved off the initiates' bodies, and they are then led to sit in one corner of the shelter, surrounded by adult men, who provide moral and spiritual support during the ordeal. The circumciser sings out *Matang' ana*, an ancient term for initiation, while the surrounding crowd responds *simba yaluma ng'ombe,* "the lion bites the cow." When the cutting is complete, the circumciser gathers together the bloodied hides they have been seated on, as well as the foreskins, and disposes of them discreetly. In part, the action is intended to hide these from witches, who might try to impair the young boys' later sexuality.

Over the next month relatives and kin visit the boys in the initiation camp. Allegorical songs are sung on these occasions, as in these examples:

> I thought it was a rhinoceros, but it was only the leaves of the wild palm [initiation was not as bad as initially feared].

> Guts have pain and I bore a child [there is pain in the act, but also reward at the birth of a child; i.e., the boys have been morally reborn].

Beidelman gives emphasis to the fact that life in the initiates' camp is the most uncomfortable and threatening experience in a boy's life to date. He has never before experienced so much physical pain and been in such an alarming situation, surrounded each nightfall by the threatening sounds of nocturnal animal life that childhood stories associate with witches and other dangerous beings. At the end of the healing period the boys return to their homes for a day of dancing, beer drinking, and general celebration. The following day they are renamed to mark their reentry into normal village life and to mark their new status as young adult men.

Kaguru girls are initiated soon after their first menstruation, and because of this, they are usually initiated separately rather than in groups. Beidelman (1997: 163) writes:

> Kaguru initiation of girls aims to educate them in proper sexual and domestic behavior. . . . Girls are taught about sexual relations, about proper sexual etiquette and comportment, but also about the special care that women must take regarding menstruation and pregnancy. . . . They say that the central feature of a girl's initiation is 'cooling,' *(imhosa)*, that is, subduing and controlling their new sexuality. . . . Menstruation itself is considered a hot *(moto)*, disturbing activity, a source of pollution and potential disorder.

At the time of her first menstruation a girl lives in seclusion in her mother's home, typically for as long as a month. She can venture outside the hut only to relieve herself. Beidelman learned that in the past, seclusion could last as long as six months. During this time she is pampered with food to enhance her feminine qualities. Kaguru men are expressly prohibited from entering the homestead while she is in seclusion.

After a night of feasting the young girl is formally initiated via an operation that entails slicing away portions of the labia. She returns to her mother's hut while the wounds heal, and when she finally reemerges into public, she is acknowledged as a marriageable woman.

Beidelman (1997: 174–180) offers a summary of what he regards as the most important differences between Kaguru female and male initiation. First, female initiation is biologically determined, whereas male initiation is socially constructed. Second, male initiation is inherently more violent and painful than is the case for females. Third, male initiation takes place outside the boundaries of normal society, while female initiation is entirely a domestic affair. On the fourth distinction, I cite Beidelman at some length. He argues that these distinctive ways of culturally altering the body denote contrasting dimensions of Kaguru sexuality:

> Kaguru boys undergo ceremonies that expose and assault the body. . . . Circumcision itself is such an act, since it exposes something vital that was previously undisclosed: the immediate and specific focus of erotic pleasure in the male body, the glans. . . . In contrast, Kaguru girls are introduced to a sexuality that should not be exposed and that ultimately cannot be clearly revealed. The central locus of their sexual pleasure, the clitoris, is not altered. It remains an element that intrudes into and retreats from sight, while their fertility, their wombs, remain mysterious and never guaranteed to yield pregnancies. (Beidelman, 1997: 177)

TIV BODIES

The Tiv of northern Nigeria became well known in the anthropological literature through a series of ethnographic monographs and
numerous scholarly articles written by the American anthropologists
Laura and Paul Bohannan. The Tiv comprise one of the largest non-
Muslim societies in this region of Africa, numbering over 1 million individuals. Paul Bohannan characterized the Tiv as a people of very independent mind, "surely one of the most ethnocentric people in the world"
(Bohannan, 1988 [1965]: 516). To illustrate the point, Bohannan relates that a Tiv man approached the first European to visit their country and asked if it were true, as they had been told, that Europeans
were immortal. The European answered in the affirmitive: yes, Europeans were immortal. His Tiv inquisitor then shot him in the chest
with an arrow. As the foreigner fell to his death, the Tiv assassin turned
to his friends and remarked that he really didn't believe it.

Traditionally, Tiv were cultivators. Because of their favorable geo-
graphical location, Tiv grew yams, millet, and sorghum in quantities
far beyond their subsistence needs. Since Tiv country lies in a region of
endemic sleeping sickness, they had no cattle but kept herds of sheep
and goats in considerable number. The basic feature of Tiv social organization is the patrilocal extended family, headed by the eldest adult
male. Tiv are well known in the anthropological literature for their system of patrilineal lineages—descendents of men who collectively share
common male ancestors. Ultimately, in Tiv thought, all the different
patrilineages in Tiv country can trace common male ancestry to their
founding ancestor, known (not surprisingly) as Tiv. Tiv marriage was
polygynous, and most adult men were married to two or three women
simultaneously. In any homestead, therefore, there is a dense cluster-
ing of patrilineally related kin, and a child grows up surrounded by a
large circle of close family.

According to Bohannan, Tiv do not have any formal initiation ceremonies. Males are circumcised, but this can occur at seven years of age
or well into adolescence. As he writes (1988 [1965]: 531), "Circumcision
must, by Tiv definition, precede adult status, but does not thereby create it." This interpretation is open to question, since circumcised males
are also organized into age-grades or age-statuses, which have important political, economic, and legal functions. Nonetheless, the traditional practice of Tiv facial and body scarification is analogous to a form
of initiation, wherein the body becomes the canvas for the cultural definition of masculine and feminine gender.

The Tiv body aesthetic takes a number of different forms and
entails differing degrees of body transformation. Some of these are

temporary, while others are carved into the skin for life. These include oiling and coloring the skin and filing and chipping teeth, in addition to permanent scarification. Women and men oil their bodies: for the Tiv, a glistening skin is both attractive and alluring. Camwood ash is also used as a cosmetic.

The most dramatic form of body decoration is scarification, and different forms and styles socially distinguish generations of women and men. Indeed, Bohannan may have missed the point that body scarification has a definitive role in engendering the body and that this serves as a key Tiv medium in differentiating the female and male form. I will return to this point shortly.

Total body scarification, a form of body adornment especially sought by women, may often take twenty-five years to complete. Bohannan (1988: 82) writes,

> I once asked a group of Tiv with whom I was discussing scarifica-
> tion whether it was not exceedingly painful. They turned on me as
> if I had missed the entire point—as, indeed, I had. 'Of course,' one
> of them said, 'of course it is painful. What girl would look at a man
> if his scars had not cost him pain?'

Although Bohannan does not provide extensive exegetical interpretation of Tiv scarification, Lincoln (1981) has examined the practice in detail, and his insights call for mention here.

Lincoln does not assert that the Bohannans failed to appreciate the ritual nature of Tiv scarification; instead, he raises the problematic question of what, in fact, constitutes ritual? Anthropologists and other scholars have written thousands of essays and hundreds of books on rituals of such-and-such among the so-and-so, but rarely in this literature does one find the local vernacular for ritual. The term *ritual* connotes a kind of behavior that is standard, formal, repetitive, and always the same. In fact, there are few behaviors of this kind in human social experience. Conversely, our living days are full of repetitive forms of behavior (waking at six in the morning, taking a shower, reading a newspaper, driving to work) that we, at least, would not think to call "ritual behavior" (see, e.g., Goffman, 1967; Leach, 1966; Miner, 1956; Turner, 1969).

In one sense standardized norms, procedures, and protocol guide all of social existence, so that social life itself could be conceived of as an unending ritual. Most anthropologists would respond by suggesting that ritual behavior differs from practical and pragmatic behavior in a fundamental way. Rituals transcend the immediate world by making symbolic reference to things beyond the obvious.

This brings us back to Lincoln's basic point and Bohannan's assertion that Tiv have no form of initiation (something that would make them peculiar in relation to the majority of sub-Saharan African societies). The Tiv case of body modification is important and interesting precisely because it raises this methodological problem. Another way to put the matter is in these terms: who created gender identity for the Sambia, the Wogoo, or the Kaguru: their anthropological interpreters or the people themselves?

Occasionally Tiv refer to female body scarification as "the circumcision of women." They do not consciously refer to it as a form of initiation. They likewise argue that male circumcision has no religious or symbolic connotations. A native ethnographer (East, 1965) of the Tiv suggests that Tiv elders were not always eager to share their knowledge with white foreigners, so a reliable, factual interpretation of the practice may still await future research. Lincoln's argument and interpretation is dramatic, resonating clearly with other features of Tiv culture and social organization. He views female scarification as the creation of a three-dimensional, living archive of patrilineal history and collective mythology, here adorned across a woman's body. Straight lines and concentric circles that are carved into a woman's abdomen—centered on the navel—represent the past history of a lineage and the way it will grow in the future. Straight lines image descent, while circular patterns, like ripples in a pond, promise the growth of the lineage in the future. Lincoln suggests that a woman's navel marks the point of her own birth and origin and does not need elaboration: "At puberty, however, it takes on new significance as the vital center where life will be formed, and at that moment it becomes the center and starting point for the symbolic design that makes a girl into a woman" (1981: 47). Lincoln's interpretation is enhanced by the fact that Tiv women regard these scars as both signs of fertility and the promise of its realization. The scars inscribed on a woman's abdomen at the time of puberty imitate, and thus recall, the fundamental, patrilineal basis of Tiv society. These make her

> the guardian of fertility and well-being, heir of the past and creator
> of the future. The scars themselves are simultaneously the means
> of her transformation and the visible mark that this transforma-
> tion has been completed, making each girl a woman and a sacred
> object for all to see. (Lincoln, 1981: 49)

It may be with the Tiv that we have an ethnographic case in which initiation and body transformation serve a function that is not perceived in this way from the local perspective. But that would not make them peculiar in relation to billions of other human beings.

For example, few people in North America would consciously and immediately suggest to a foreign anthropologist that graduation from high school is a form of initiation, that boot camp is a form of initiation, or that reaching the age of twenty-one is a form of initiation. Yet each of these social experiences share qualities in common. They all mark the attainment of a novel status and imbue individuals with new authority, responsibility and power. As with the four ethnographic cases discussed, they likewise change the social personality and public persona of individuals. Importantly, they are also occasions where the private body is culturally costumed.

LOOKING BACK

This chapter began with a thumbnail sketch of Van Gennep's original and innovative perspective on transition rituals and rites of passage, followed by a reference to Beidelman's suggestion that women are more deeply beings of their biology than men. To some, this statement would appear to be a clear example of male bias and chauvinism. It is important to remember that the observation was made in regard to the cultural construction of gender stereotypes, in relation to the human body. The specific intention was to point out that women's physical and sexual maturity—like their role in childbirth—is self-evident, thus requiring little cultural elaboration. From this perspective, therefore, the more anomalous and ambiguous matter of male sexuality invites greater attention and cultural elaboration. An issue of this sort requires commentary from multiple perspectives.

An obvious matter to emphasize at the outset is that four ethnographic cases cannot provide a basis for broad generalization, nor were they cited for that purpose. However, forms of initiation such as these involve structure, gender, and status. Cross-culturally, initiation rituals share so many features in common that they appear to form what has recently been called a polythetic class of the human imagination. The phrase *polythetic classification* first gained currency in anthropological thinking in 1975 (see Needham, 1975). *Polythetic* is a compound of the Greek *poly* (many) and *thetos* (arrangement). It refers to the fact that all members of a particular system of classification do not necessarily share all features in common. By example, some tables have four legs, some three, and others only one. Regardless, the word *table* denotes a particular kind of furniture. The use of the term in the present context emphasizes the point that while the cultural content of initiation ceremonies varies enormously, their underlying form is consistently the same. Said in other terms, forms of initiation have many more features in common than do the societies in which they are found (see also Needham, 1963). Why is this so?

Power, domination, and hierarchy are universal dimensions of human social life. These phenomena vary only in association with population density and modes of production. The Mbuti of the Ituri rain forest and political bureaucrats in Western societies live in equally political environments. The difference between them is purely a matter of scale. In a veiled sense what we speak of as political behavior is

in fact a matter of social control. Human bodies are controlled in all
public places, sometimes by violent force. In the context of initiation,
bodies are not typically controlled by brute force (the Sambian case is
an obvious exception), but by subtle cultural recipes. To be initiated
means to be regimented and controlled, to be accepted and at the same
time to be dominated. That the definition and control of sexuality is so
commonly a focus of ritual attention is testament to the social need to
regulate this powerful, so-called natural force. In very simple terms,
initiation rituals impose cultural rules to define and regulate sexuality
and, thus, gender.

The human species appears to be unique in this regard. As far as
we can be certain, there is no other animate form that teaches, and
thereby constrains, reproductive or any other form of sexual behavior.
Primates control sexual behavior through dominance hierarchies, but
the human plan is subtler. Cultural designs have a powerful impact on
sexuality. As noted in the last chapter, in traditional China the female
foot became a sexual fetish; in North America the female breast
attracts similar attention; in a number of societies of southern Africa,
women artificially elongated their labia as a means of enhancing their
sexuality and attractiveness. Rituals of initiation construct and define
a particular focus of human sexuality. Forms of initiation are universal,
by this reasoning, because controlling sexuality and the body are universal requirements of social life.

Bettelheim's arguments are more problematic, as is any effort at
cross-cultural, Freudian interpretation. Do men really desire to be like
females? This is probably as doubtful as Freud's assertion of female
penis envy. Do men deeply wish they could give birth? Do men really
wish that their sexual organ resembled the female counterpart? I rather
doubt this. Would they want to control female sexuality and birth? There
are many instances that could be cited to answer this question affirma-
tively. But in any case, the extant range of human sexual behavior is too
broad to make definitive generalizations about its object and purpose.
Women tend to desire men as sexual partners just as men tend to desire
women. One of the primary functions of initiation ceremonies is to chan-
nel this intention and desire in a culturally prescribed direction.

Another objection to Bettelheim's interpretation, which later in
his life he recanted, is that he, like many other Freudians, regarded the
behavior of primitive people as a manifestation of neurotic behavior as
witnessed in his own society. Assuming as we now can that there is in
fact a unity to the human psyche, the problems humans confront in
defining and regulating sexuality are likewise universal. The plasticity
of human sexual behavior is concurrently evidence of the powerful way
in which culture determines this so-called natural behavior.

Another of Bettelheim's interpretations invites further reflection.
The subtitle of his 1954 book is *Puberty Rites and the Envious Male*.

Though many human societies are structured by patriarchal ideologies, the reproduction of social life is commonly a feminine rather than masculine undertaking. In this light, and in sympathy with Beidelman's argument, male initiation ceremonies may be regarded as a means to assert symbolically a male equivalent to feminine reproductive creativity. Sambian initiation again supports this interpretation. Further, cultural practices such as the couvade can be cited as an illustration of this point. The common cultural practice of inflicting painful and bloody transformations of the male member suggests a clear analog to the natural process of female menstruation.

In a very different way, initiation also has a powerful effect on the human desire for belonging, being accepted and recognized as a member of a group of common identity. This urge most likely has its roots in our evolutionary history. The process of physical transformation is at the same time a process of psychological transformation. To experience trauma, anxiety, or pain as an individual is an experience that can be very alienating. To survive such ordeals collectively is fundamentally a different experience. The Sambian masculine transformation is one case in point. Here initiation is not only a matter of social control but is also a collective expression of masculine identity. That male initiation is most commonly a group phenomenon is notable in this regard. For the Sambia, the Nuer, or the Maasai, survival in the precolonial world often entailed small-scale feuding and warfare, where survival or success required male solidarity. In notable contrast to these examples are the initiation ceremonies of Tiv, Kaguru, and Hofriyat women, where creative (rather than destructive) potential is focused on the single individual.

Rites of passage and forms of initiation should be understood in their full social context, as "total social phenomena" in the words of Marcel Mauss (see Beidelman, 1997). They are occasions of deep personal transformation and also signs of public ownership. At one and the same time, they reconfigure personal identity and represent the value of collective identity. Indeed, the initiated body is the most salient and powerful of the society that constructs it. The body becomes a model of and also for society (see Geertz, 1973).

This brings the interpretation back to Beidelman's argument. Women are no more "deeply beings of their biology" than men are. Both are quite clearly biosocial beings. But the ethnographic record does indeed suggest that there is for men (and for women?) a greater degree of ambivalence and ambiguity about masculine identity. Another way to state the matter is to suggest that what women are capable of naturally, men can only do through the manipulation of cultural symbols.

Chapter Five

Now and Then
Technology and the Body

During the past year or so, as my ideas for this monograph took a clearer form, students, friends, and colleagues occasionally asked what I actually planned to write about. The habitual response became something like "a broad anthropological overview of culture and the human body." Colleagues typically responded, "Oh yeah. The body is a hot topic these days." This may be true, but the more important fact to bear in mind is that for human beings, concern with the human body has been a hot topic since the time our species developed intelligence and self-consciousness. Hundreds of thousands of human generations have manipulated the body for medical, aesthetic, personal, and collective reasons. The body has long been an object of cultural, and thus technical, attention and elaboration. What has changed within our lifetimes is the *magnitude* of technological modifications of the body, and the degree to which the body has become another commodity in the world of global capitalism. In the past half-century we have also increasingly lost control of our individual bodies. The modern state defines who we are, how we are born, what food we eat, what chemicals we are allowed to ingest, what kind of residences we live in, how and when we are allowed to die, and what legally can be done with our corpses. The modern body is a product of technology and impersonal bureaucracy. This should come as no surprise. The record of human cultural evolution over the past million years has made a firm and lasting impression on the human physical form. As human technologies have become more complex, the human body has become ever-more dependent on complex forms of technology.

Brief reference to labor history in North America makes this point quite clear. In the middle of the nineteenth century, farm animals performed about one half of productive labor—drawing plows and wagons and carrying people. Humans contributed about 15 percent to this effort. Emerging mechanized industries and technologies contributed 35 percent. One hundred years later, humans contributed less than 1 percent to productive labor, and machines filled in with the remaining 99 percent. In the 1850s, an individual farmer produced enough food by his own labor to feed four people on a regular basis. At the time of this writing, less than 1 percent of the labor force is involved in the production of food. Agribusiness produces food resources that feed approximately 90 percent of the world's human population. Now virtually freed from the task of producing their livelihood, members of modern society imagine they live the highest standard of living known in human history. This is an attractive but misleading myth. In the twenty-first century more people suffer from psychological stress and body compulsions than at any point in human history. Although North Americans can expect greater longevity, hundreds of thousands of older people are alive because medicines and medical technology assure their day-to-day survival. At the same time, millions of people in the third world live marginal lives in consequence of the benefits of development.

HUMAN POPULATION

As I write, the human population is larger than at any point in known history, with more than 6 billion people working through their lives. The human population is also younger than it has ever been: more people are entering adolescence than ever before. In 1798, the English economist Thomas Malthus published a book titled *Essay on the Principle of Population.* In this study he argued that as the human population continued to grow, it would eventually outpace food resources. His prediction has not yet been realized. However, at the present rate of population growth, the number of human beings will double every forty years in the future. Malthus may have been mistaken in his time, but he may just as well be right in the future. The technologies that have made this growth possible—such as hydroelectric dams, nuclear reactors, and plant pesticides—have altered global ecology in such a way that human adaptation to the earth has become more fragile at the very same time it has become technologically complex. Beginning with the earliest technology of plant and animal domestication, the global human population began to grow in a gradual manner. By the middle of the nineteenth century, a dramatic increase began. The reasons for this are complex and varied, but they are all related to human technology and the human body.

As Europeans began to settle in the New World, they brought with them domesticated plants, animals and a technological tool kit that were unknown in this part of the globe. Many indigenous people were seasonal foragers and hunters. Although domesticated beans, corn, and squash had diffused widely through North America in pre-Columbian times, the introduction of draft-animal plow agriculture resulted in food surpluses, which in turn spawned population growth—a cultural replay from southwest Asia 7,000 years before. More recently, the so-called "green revolution" of the 1960s has similar consequences in India and elsewhere in Asia, as farmers could reap as many as three harvests in a single year. The dramatic increase in field production was the direct consequence of genetic and other technological innovations in agriculture; it resulted, in turn, in a dramatic population growth.

While the revolution in food production was emerging, dramatic innovations in the diagnosis and treatment of fatal diseases continued apace. Many crowd-born diseases were eradicated during the last century, also in consequence of technologies directly affecting the human body. In short, human transformations of the physical and chemical world have resulted in longer life expectancies than at any previous moment in history. Cultural innovations have also produced new diseases. There has thus been a down side to technological manipulation of the human body. At the same time the technological capacity to promote life has advanced, so too has the human capability to end it violently.

A recent *New York Times* article reported that 180,000,000 human beings died as a consequence of warfare in the twentieth century. We are the only species that systematically slaughters its members in large numbers on a more or less regular basis. For the modern nation-state, the human body is merely a resource to be deployed to advance strategic or nationalistic ends, as evidenced by the 1944 D day invasion on the shores of Normandy, the savage destruction of human life in Southeast Asia in the 1960s and 1970s, and the truly inhuman sacrifice of human bodies during the Iranian-Iraqi war of the 1990s. Perhaps the demonic perversions of the Nazi state provide the most-telling evidence of this tragic human flaw.

CULTURE AND REPRODUCTION

The regulation of human populations provides another perspective on the ways in which contemporary technology regulates the body, as well as life itself. Reproduction, of course, is a fundamental requisite for the perpetuation of a species. Human cultures have invented diverse ways to control this natural process, from imposing food taboos on infants and pregnant mothers to differential childcare and infanticide. So-called "traditional" practices have taken new form in recent decades as medical technology has transformed the "natural" process of human gestation and birth. Technology provides new options. For example, in rural north India anthropologist Barbara Miller (1987: 110; see also Miller, 1981, 1984, 1993) noted:

> In one village I went into the house to examine a young girl and I found that she had an advanced case of tuberculosis. I asked the mother why she hadn't done something sooner about the girl's condition because now, at this stage, the treatment would be very expensive. The mother replied, ". . . then let her die. I have another daughter." At the time, the two daughters sat nearby listening, one with tears streaming down her face.

As the technique of amniocentesis has become more common, parents have greater freedom in deciding whether a fetus should be brought to term or aborted because of its sex or physical characteristics. In societies such as China and India, where sons are highly favored over daughters, this technique can multiply the effects of traditional custom. Another stunning fact is that human beings are the only mammalian species that can reproduce without copulating, a fact that clearly demonstrates the way in which technology and cultural invention affect the human body.

In his recent historical study of the evolution of human contraception, Allyn (1999) suggests this technology has transformed both birthing practices and marital relations (see also Tiger, 2000). He demonstrates a clear correlation between increased use of contraceptive devices and an increase in the number of single-parent families. He estimates that as many as one third of the babies born in industrialized societies have single mothers as the only parent. The so-called sexual revolution was largely a consequence of nonreproductive technologies, and the wide availability of diverse contraceptive technologies is likewise associated with a host of moral and ethical dilemmas.

Among these issues, the polar debate between "pro-life" and "pro-choice" factions has generated the most public attention in the United States. Underlying this rancor, however, is the more fundamental question of who owns and controls a woman's sexual and reproductive capabilities: a religious tradition, the state, the federal government, or herself? At the time of writing, when an unwanted or unexpected pregnancy occurs, "choice" is a function of public law rather than individual persuasion. The so-called "morning after pill" is readily available in France, and its use has just been legalized in the United States. If swallowing a pill, rather than an outpatient procedure, can terminate a pregnancy, doesn't this answer the question about body ownership? Perhaps not: as long as state and federal law are able to prohibit this technology, a woman's body is not her own but is the property of the state. Keeping poor women pregnant is a very powerful way of keeping them poor (see Andrews, 1999; Brody, 1998; Brundage, 1987; Connery, 1977; Davis, 1988; Finkle and Macintosh, 1994; Ginsburg and Rapp,

1991; Hartman, 1982; Mohr, 1978; Petchesky, 1990; Ramsey, 1970a; Rorrik, 1978; Strong, 1977; Walters and Palmer, 1996; Warnock, 1985).

Technologies for regulating reproduction are a commonplace in contemporary North America, but it is easy to forget that efforts at wide-scale population control—or destruction—are hardly novel. The ancient Greeks had firm ideas about the natural order of society: there were those who were naturally superior and therefore privileged and those who were naturally slaves, in addition to the ever-threatening barbarians beyond the boundaries of civilized existence. Following Columbus and then Cortés in the New World, Europeans claimed that it was their God-given right to slaughter or enslave indigenous people since they were neither Christian, Caucasian, nor civilized. At best, they were considered cannibals (see Arens, 1979).

Yet none of these people had a scientific rationale for their programs of human extermination. In Western thought, this originated in the work of Francis Galton, who first applied the notion of survival of the fittest to human rather than animal behavior. Galton suggested that the human race could be improved if certain favorable qualities were deliberately bred into, and others removed from, the human gene pool. Galton's ideas merged with those of the nineteenth-century sociologist Herbert Spencer and spread the seeds for what would become known as social Darwinism. This ideology suggested that more advanced societies were clearly more fit in a Darwinian sense and thus had the right to dominate or exterminate less fit populations. This was clearly a useful ideology in the context of imperialism and colonialism, since it provided a rationale for rampant Euroamerican racism and exploitation.

From this intellectual climate the eugenics movement was born. This was an effort to remove inferior races from the gene pool. A main player in this effort was the American biologist C. B. Davenport. With support from the Carnegie Foundation, in 1904 he began research on human inheritance and genealogy. His efforts were also lavishly supported through the personal philanthropy of some of the wealthiest Americans at the time, including Mrs. Edward Harriman and John D. Rockefeller (Jonsen, 1998). In 1910, Davenport opened the Eugenics Record Office, which, over the next thirty years, collected reams of information on North American families and "racial" groups. The aim was to prove that certain races were inherently inferior to others. Out of the vast data base amassed by Davenport and his colleagues emerged claims that epilepsy, criminality and alcoholism, along with other undesirable social traits, were genetically inherited (see Jonsen 1998: 169). (It is critically important to recall here that at the turn of the twentieth century, anything that carried with it the aura of scientific discovery was likened to divine truth. Darwin's theory of evolution had effectively made God a question, and anything that carried with it the tag "science" was an incontestable truth.) Many in the eugenics movement were particularly concerned about the alleged problems caused by the great influx of what they called "blood" from peoples of Mediterranean Europe. It was asserted that these people were prone to crimes of larceny, kidnapping, assault, murder, rape, and general sexual immorality. Major public figures, such as Theodore Roosevelt, Harvard President Charles Eliot, and the Reverend Harry Emerson Fosdick (the most popular preacher of the era), enthusiastically espoused eugenics doctrines (Jonsen, 1998: 170).

In 1914 the American Breeder's Association published a report titled *On The Best Practical Means of Cutting Off Defective Germ Plasma in the American Population.* The association recommended that America should regard germ plasma as its own possession and recommended forced sterilization for the feebleminded, insane, criminalistic, epileptic, inebriate, diseased, blind, deaf, deformed, and dependent (Jonsen, 1998: 170). The chilling suggestion emerges that Nazism was at least indirectly an American-bred product. By 1930, thirty-six American states had laws providing for the sterilization of criminals (Jonsen, 1998). Only a few years later Hitler demanded that Jews should be sterilized and exterminated.

FASHIONS OF CONCEPTION

As Western societies have developed technologies to inhibit conception, they have also developed novel technologies to refine conception. As noted previously, by the middle of the twentieth century, human beings became the singular mammalian species that could reproduce without copulating. For some, this was a major step toward an ideal world. To shark-feeding lawyers, the legal issues attending artificial reproduction became an unmapped oil field of litigation and profit. For science fiction writers it was merely the realization of the human imagination. For NASA planners working on deep space endeavors, there was the promise of interstellar missions that might last hundreds of years. (Since the human life span is so short and the time required for deep space exploration is so vast that computer-controlled breeding across hundreds of generations became a plausible solution for supplying a crew for these expeditions.) But for our species as a whole, the emergence of artificial reproduction pointed us one step further down the road to social and technological slavery. The human genetic form has been mapped, and animal cloning will soon be a standard laboratory procedure. The looming moral issues are ominous. Many North Americans entered this age inheriting a tradition in which marriage was monogamous and life-long, abortion was never an option, and interspecies organ transplants were unthinkable. Yet it is probable that patients needing heart surgery within the next twenty years will not have to rely on a pacemaker. Instead, a pig's heart, largely identical to the human organ, and farmed for this purpose, will serve as an implant.

In the 1950s frozen human sperm was first used to fertilize a human ovum. Fifteen years later in vitro conception had become a standard procedure. Human beings were produced in petri dishes. Our ancestors probably could not understand this. One can now go on line to access a Web site advertising eggs from fashion models. The choices include the height, weight, hair color, and breast size of selected individuals. Nothing is mentioned about their personal history. Rather, the hype is generated to convince potential buyers that they can become the parents of a culturally idealized form, at a cost ranging from $50,000 to $200,000 dollars. The man who maintains this Web site claims 20 percent commission for each sale. For those more concerned with parenting than with birthing fashion model clones, a supermarket approach to embryo purchase is emerging. Kolata (1997) writes about a 47-year-old woman from New Jersey who was pregnant with triplets: "But the babies bear no resemblance to her or her husband. . . . Instead, they are growing from ready-made embryos that the family selected and paid for at the Columbia-Presbyterian Medical Center in Manhattan." According to the same source, this form of birthing technology has resulted in unknown numbers of births in recent years.

Until recently, the law of supply and demand made the female product more expensive, since eggs are produced in fewer numbers and at a slower rate than sperm. Recent technological innovations have begun to alter the market principle, as well as biological facts. Since the process of ovulation follows a cyclical, monthly pattern, dead women cannot produce eggs on demand. Dead men, on the other hand, can produce sperm. As Andrews (1999) observed, in July of 1995, a young man died suddenly and unexpectedly in a California hospital. Within hours, his wife and her family were on the telephone with a urologist at Century Hospital in Los Angeles. They asked him to meet them at the morgue so that they could collect sperm from her dead husband's corpse. Thirty hours after his death sperm were extracted from his body. Four years later they were used to fertilize the wife. Sperm can now be collected from a dead man by a procedure known as electroejaculation. An instrument resembling a cattle prod is inserted into the rectum of the dead body. Following a powerful electric shock, the technique produces an involuntary ejaculation. Sperm is collected to be used for fertilization in the short term or frozen for future use or sale. According to Andrews, this procedure is now so common that the American Society of Reproductive Medicine has developed a protocol, known as Posthumous Reproduction, to define the parameters of its use.

This procedure, like many other recent innovations in medical technology, raises a number of moral and ethical dilemmas that were previously unimagined. Some have suggested that collecting sperm in this way is only a short step away from rape; here, however, it is the rape of a dead man, possibly against his will. An analogous conundrum is provided by the case of a comatose woman who was raped in a nursing home and later gave birth (Miller, 1998). How might a dead man feel if he had the knowledge that he had become a father, through no effort of his own, to produce a child he might not have wanted to sire? Likewise, how might a clinically dead woman react to the fact that her dead body was used a birthing machine? As I will discuss later, the United States Supreme Court has ruled that a comatose individual cannot be forced to accept life-sustaining treatment in the effort to artificially prolong life. Given the technique of electroejaculation, the question becomes whether or not a dead person should be able to contribute to life-creating treatments. In other words, once we are dead, what are the moral and legal issues regarding reproduction against our will?

Questions of this sort are novel, but inevitable, given the fact that the business of medical technology is driven by market forces, rather than by medical reasons per se. When a new medical procedure is invented, it is typically promoted as a medical necessity. Annas (1998) argues that new medical technology is the mother of medical necessity. From this perspective, the marketing of sperm and eggs is best understood as a new form of conspicuous consumption: the genetically groomed child is like the hottest new BMW or a posh address. Annas (1998: 21) suggests, "Treating infertility by using the new reproductive technologies has become a multibillion-dollar business that is itself dominated not by the medical ideology of the best interests of patients and their children, but by the market ideology of profit maximization under the guise of reproductive liberty."

ORGANS FOR HARVEST AND SALE

Following the discovery of the four major blood groups in 1900, blood transfusion became a standard technique in Western medical practice. Medical studies of the casualties suffered in World War I and World War II led to a better understanding of the genetic nature of immunological barriers to organ, skin, and other forms of body transplants. One of the first successful organ transplants was performed in 1954, when the surgeons Joseph Murray and John Merrill removed and implanted a kidney between twin brothers (Jonsen 1998: 21). During the decade of 1954 to 1964, "more than 600 renal transplants between living persons were performed in the United States, Canada, Britain and France" (Jonsen 1998: 197). Approximately 50 percent of patients survived for at least two years after the procedure. Dramatic medical history was made in 1967 when Dr. Christian Barnard of South Africa performed the first successful human heart transplant. During this dramatic surgery, Barnard held in his hand the still-beating heart of a twenty-two-year-old woman, seriously injured in a car accident the previous day, and sewed it into the chest of a fifty-five-year-old man, whose heart had ceased to function adequately. Human organ transplant operations have become commonplace since this time, and mention of an artificial heart no longer raises eyebrows or causes confusion. The practice of organ harvesting has replaced this dated usage.

Organ harvesting most often occurs in a situation where a patient has been declared brain dead. Jonsen (1998: 205) estimated that in 1985 there were at least 200,000 people in North America needing immediate organ transplants, with a waiting list more than twice as long. Capitalism being what it is, many people have offered to sell their organs to the national and global market. An interspecies market has also emerged through the attempt to implant chimpanzee and baboon hearts for human use (see Blumstein and Sloan, 1989; Calebresi and Bobbitt, 1978; Caplan, 1992; Carrel and Lindburgh, 1938; Fox and Swazey, 1976; Gaylin, 1974; Leach, 1970; Moore, 1964; Titmus, 1971; Veatch, 1976).

The modern body is no longer an entity unto itself, but rather a module, with interchangeable parts and components. As Scott (1981: 3) suggests, "Dead or alive, the human body now has an intrinsic value. To be precise, the value inheres not in the body as an entity, but in its component parts." This circumstance directly confronts and challenges our modern sense of individuality and identity, which is first and foremost based on a sense of the inherent singularity of our individual bodies.

WHO GETS THE GOODS? AN APPLIED DILEMMA

As part of a class presentation for a seminar on anthropology and the body, a number of my students prepared an exercise in what they termed anthro-ethics—a problem of deciding who among a range of people would be given a new body organ in a time of need. To set the ground rules, students indicated that all the candidates for this simulated heart transplant operation would have equal access to a hospital, that they would all have health insurance, and that they would apply for treatment at the same time.

The first applicant was Mrs. Malanya Sababski, a seventy-five-year-old immigrant from Poland, living in suburban Chicago. Her only daughter and son-in-law died in a car accident, leaving her as the primary caretaker and guardian of her three young grandchildren. Mrs. Sabanski was a heavy smoker.

Second on the list was Juan Pablo Elizando, a twenty-year-old Cuban-American college student studying in the United States on a full scholarship. If his academic work were successful, he would be the first in his family to attain a college degree. Juan was diagnosed with a fatal heart murmur after he collapsed on the field during a soccer match. He is currently facing charges of sexual assault by college officials.

Ann Whitehall is a forty-five-year-old mother of two living in Greenwich, Connecticut. She is actively involved with the PTA at her children's school and is on the board of directors of the Arts Association of Fairfield County. Each year she serves as chair of a local art auction, all proceeds of which are donated to research on children's cancer. Mrs. Whitehall has a history of abusing diet pills.

Padre Phil Johnson, aged forty-seven, is a prominent missionary from Salt Lake City, Utah. His career has focused on "bringing religion" to people in remote areas of Central and South America and improving health care techniques for indigenous peoples. He has been quoted as saying that his life calling is to "improve the conditions of the less fortunate of the world." He is married and has seven children.

Malika Jefferson is a thirty-year-old African-American woman who has a congenital heart condition. She is widowed and the mother of three young children and lives in Atlanta, Georgia. Mrs. Jefferson works for the United States Postal Service and also works part-time in a local coffee shop to earn extra money for her children's after-school activities.

Michael Paralones is thirty-nine. He lives in New York City but was born in the Philippines. He teaches dance and is highly regarded as a choreographer. Mr. Paralones lives in Soho in Manhattan with his partner, Danny, and their three cats. Danny and Michael are in the process of adopting a Filipino baby. They serve as co-chairs of a state-funded AIDS research project in New York.

Kimberly Davis, an eighteen-year-old-woman from Hanover, Indiana, has just given birth to her first child. She is living on welfare. Kimberly became pregnant after she ran away from home, when she was living on the street for about a year. She recently enrolled in a program to complete her high school equivalency and hopes to enter a nearby vocational school so she can pursue a career in cosmetology.

These are fictional constructions, but they provide an authentic cross-section of contemporary citizens. How would attending doctors, health professionals, and legal aides decide who among them should receive the only heart available for transplant? Who plays God in this circumstance? Who do you think is the most deserving? Students in my course decided this way (the number one indicates first priority): (1) Malika Jefferson; (2) Kimberly Davis; (3) Ann Whitehall; (4) Phil Johnson; (5) Malanya Sabanski; (6) Juan Elizando; (7) Michael Paralones. The choice was not easy: it consumed two hours of heated debate, but in the end, the ranking was unanimous. In reality, the ranking doesn't matter at all. After number one, the rest are dead anyway. Malika Jefferson was selected because she was the person who faced the greatest challenges and needs in her situation of life: an African-American woman, single, with two jobs, trying to make ends meet. In the real world it is far more likely that the fictional Ann Whitehall would be awarded the treasured heart. As an affluent, white female, social status, rather than medical need, would carry the day.

TECHNOLOGY, LIFE, AND DEATH

"The invention of two medical machines, the ventilator and the respirator, plus the skill of the transplant surgeon, have forced us to change our perception of death, and have illuminated our inability to say unequivocally what death is, or conversely, what life is" (Scott 1981: 141). Life is the absence of death, and death is the absence of life. At the very moment human life begins, so too does death. We are alone as a species in possessing the irrefutable knowledge of our eventual mortality. The creation myths of thousands of human cultures are based on this primordial dichotomy. Time and again, humans have imagined that life began with the origin of death. Timelessness was then radically transformed by an act of human agency. Many myths suggest that when human beings first acted self-consciously, they brought about the conditions of their own demise. In the hardball world of modernity, mythical narratives wilt in the face of state and federal laws. The definition of life and death are matters of civil legislation. Of course, it has not always been this way.

During the Christian Middle Ages, there emerged an art of dying, or *ars moriendi* (see Jonsen, 1998: 233), a ritualized preparation to encounter one's creator and redeemer. Physicians at the time had relatively little part to play in the final drama of human life and death. In earlier times, Greek physicians were admonished to ignore those who were "overmastered by their disease" (1998: 233). In the sixteenth century Francis Bacon coined the term *euthanasia* to mean a good or easy death. But until the emergence of state-controlled medical practice in the middle of the nineteenth century, the occasion of death was largely a matter of personal and family consideration. In the 1940s and 1950s in North America, when medical practice became increasingly regulated by bureaucratic mandates, medical science took the form of denying death. Medicine became a means of controlling the body through technology (1998: 234). The body had become a pseudomachine, not a holistic entity: a series of interconnecting parts that could be maintained and changed as needed. To Jonsen (1998) this "sea change" raised two novel questions: (1) how was clinical death to be defined and determined, and (2) when, and under what circumstances, should artificial life-support systems be maintained or withdrawn?

The respirator placed the hand of God in the hands of humans. A technology that could artificially prolong life functions of the body confounded the definition of death. (The exact physiology of death continues to be a mystery.) With this new technology, a person could theoretically live forever in a vegetative state, even while he or she was brain dead. Realizing what profound moral dilemmas had emerged, in the late 1950s an elite group of medical practitioners sought council from Pope Pius XII. It was his view that only "ordinary means" should be used to preserve and maintain human life. His religious authority also concluded that it was not possible to define or control death (Jonsen, 1998: 237). Medical practitioners then wondered whether or not the body of a brain dead person might be regarded as a cadaver, and thus the source of organs for possible transplant. In short, the technology of the respirator forced the medical world to provide a new definition of death. In 1968, an ad hoc committee met at the Harvard Medical School to define medical procedure in this situation and concluded that the condition of death may include the status of irreversible coma (Jonsen, 1998: 238). And so the way was cleared to harvest organs from bodies in this condition. Legally, transplant specialists would therefore not be regarded as murderers, but simply as technicians, performing a normal procedure.

The Harvard committee's report gained federal recognition and sanction by a presidential commission in 1980. The latter group produced a document titled the Uniform Determination of Death Act, which declared that any individual who has sustained either irreversible cessation of circulatory and respiratory functions or irreversible cessation of all functions of the entire brain, including the brain stem, is dead (Jonsen, 1998: 243). This creates a bemusing paradox for the modern body: we have the right to forego artificial life-sustaining treatment but are not allowed the option to take our own lives. The federal government and the medical community thus control our lives and bodies.

And so it is for the newborn. As noted, human reproduction can now be an entirely artificial process. When the incubator was first introduced in the early 1960s, the technology was widely hailed as yet another stunning achievement of Western science and medicine. However, it was soon observed that some premature babies who were housed in incubators developed a condition known as idiopathic respiratory distress syndrome. Their lungs do not grow in pace with the rest of their body. As a result, babies tended to in this manner may later develop chronic lung disease as well as neurological complications that can lead to mental retardation (Jonsen, 1998: 245).

One of the most telling narratives regarding the sacrifice of the body to medical technology and the state is offered by the case of Baby Doe (Jonsen, 1998: 249). This involved a child who was born in Bloomington, Indiana, in 1982. Through prenatal tests, the parents learned that their expected child had Down's syndrome, complicated by a con-

dition known as esophageal atresia—a blockage in the esophagus that
is common in such cases. The attending doctor wanted to perform surgery to correct the problem, but the parents would not give their
approval. The doctor then filed suit for a court-ordered surgery. The
Indiana court sided with the parents. It is reported that President
Ronald Reagan learned about this situation on the evening news and
ordered Richard Schweiker, his secretary of Health and Human Services, to prohibit this in the future. "The President," said Secretary Schweiker, "has instructed me to make absolutely clear to health providers
in this nation that Federal law does not allow medical discrimination
against handicapped infants" (Jonsen, 1998: 249). The message is
clear: we do not own the children we produce. Their bodies, like our
own, are the property of the medical profession and the state.

Within Western medical practice, the inevitability of death is
denied: death is regarded as professional failure. In recent years, the
body has come to be regarded as a battlefield between invading disease
and defensive technology. As Annas (1998: 45) argues:

> The military metaphor has historically had the most pervasive in-
> fluence over both the practice and financing of medicine in the
> United States. . . . Until recently, most U.S. physicians had served
> in the military. Examples are legion. Medicine is a battle against
> death. Diseases attack the body, uniformed physicians intervene.
> We are almost constantly engaged in wars on various diseases. (See
> also Douglas and Calvez, 1990; Gilman, 1987; Hunter, n.d.; Scarry,
> 1985; Slack, 1988; Sontag, 1989.)

Death is a medical defeat: it marks the failure of technology and technique. Annas (1998: 76–77) continues:

> In a market-driven economy, where physicians are producers and
> patients are consumers . . . society permits people to die when their
> bodies refuse any further input of treatment, after which they be-
> come useless not only as a producer but also as a consumer . . . and
> must be written off as a total loss. Physicians often tend to treat pa-
> tients with terminal illness aggressively for a variety of motives, in-
> cluding misplaced fear of civil litigation if they do not. Their heroic
> efforts to ward off the inevitable often compromise the quality of
> their patient's remaining life.

A failed effort to prolong life is sometimes regarded as a success,
regardless. We have all heard the phrase "The patient died, but the
operation was successful." The tragic irony of death in North America
is that people would prefer to die at home, without pain, in a relatively
short time, amidst friends, family, and loved ones. Most of us will die,
however, in state and federally regulated hospitals, slowly, in pain and
surrounded by strangers (see also Anonymous, 1968; Brooks, 1967;
Dworkin and Frey, 1998; Fletcher, 1975; Gomez, 1991; Jonsen and Gar-

land, 1992; Korein, 1978; Lyon, 1985; McCormack, 1994; Patterson, 1987; Piers, 1978; Ramsey, 1978; Reiser, 1992; Siebald, 1992; U. S. Government, 1981).

EUTHANASIA

Mortality is inevitable even though the medical profession is determined to perpetuate life: not necessarily the life of a particular individual, but life in a more abstract and philosophical sense. Again, I refer to Annas (1988: 155), who draws to attention some of the Orwellian doublespeak about medical practice: "experimentation is treatment, researchers are physicians and subjects are patients. . . . the experiment is justified as therapy, or potential therapy. But if it produces harm, it was, after all, only an experiment and was thus necessarily a success."

For these and related reasons, the American Medical Association, with the backing of state and federal legislation, has aggressively fought the legalization of euthanasia, or "peaceful death." Self-immolation denies medical practice the reason for its very existence. Concurrently, euthanasia explicitly denies the value of medical practice and experimentation. Recall that suicide is illegal in North America. As Durkheim argued, suicide is public evidence that society has failed. Terminally ill patients are not so much under the care of doctors as they are under their control. If modern society were conceived of as a low-security prison, the act of euthanasia indicates that a prisoner has escaped.

Throughout the last century medical technology and changing dietary habits in North America have played a decisive role in extending the natural life span of the human body. A longer life, however, does not guarantee a better quality of existence. Mental functions become labored; in the case of stroke, these may cease to function. Primary physical behaviors such as walking, eating, sleeping, and defecating can become difficult, stressful, and painful. For many, the so-called golden years are physically and psychologically the most demanding and difficult in life's journey. The professional and legal battle against euthanasia persists because the practice stares in contradiction to a primary ethical code of medical practice: a physician should not hasten death nor be a partner to mortality. This is a fundamental creed of Judeo-Christian theology and morality. It is simultaneously an assertion that the human body is a social, rather than an individual, possession.

Public media have made the American Dr. Jack Kevorkian the most highly recognized advocate of assisted suicide. After the popular Sunday evening television program *60 Minutes* aired a film showing Kevorkian assisting a suicide. The reaction from the American Medical Association was inflamed and direct. In a statement released after the broadcast, the American Medical Association asserted that Kevorkian was "not a physician caring for a patient, but a self-admitted zealot killing another human being to advance his own interests and ego-driven urge to martyrdom" (see Schragger, n.d.). That this association should take such a direct ad hominum stance against Kevorkian is itself worthy of comment. Similar practices are part of the day-to-day world of North American hospitals. Doctors routinely disconnect life-support systems and curtail medical prescriptions. The real issue centers on who is ultimately in control of the body and, therefore, life.

The American Medical Association recently began a program called the Care at the End of Life Campaign. Recognizing that some terminally ill patients can live on without heavy sedation, the program also emphasizes that other people may in fact need such attention precisely because the pain of imminent death is so great. An obvious question emerges: what is the real difference between the practice of terminal sedation and physician-assisted euthanasia? The consequences of either action are identical: the death of the patient. The only difference is that the courts and the federal government endorse one technique, and the other is an act of free will and choice and is therefore illegal.

THE BIRTH OF BIOETHICS

The field of bioethics has been defined as "the systematic study of the moral dimensions of the life sciences and health care, employing a variety of ethical methodologies in an interdisciplinary setting" (Jonsen, 1998: vii). In simpler terms, bioethics is concerned with what we should and should not do to the human body. This is a fairly new field of specialization, but one that is also rapidly growing, trying to keep pace with technological innovations. Jonsen traces the origins of the field to the 1947 Nuremberg Tribunal, which was organized in order to carefully examine Nazi war crimes and to investigate twenty-three physicians convicted of murder under the ruse of "medical research." At the heart of this discipline is the realization that healing and the general application of medical technology entail religious, moral, and metaphysical assumptions and the realization that transformations such as these have ethical consequences. One of its first areas of inquiry was a study that began in 1932, in Tuskegee, Alabama. Here, some 600 African-American men had been diagnosed with syphilis, though they were never informed of the fact. Instead, their medical and physical condition was monitored over a thirty-year period in an effort to understand the long-term consequences of the disease (see also Flaste, 1992; Freund, 1969; Johnson, 1990; Johnson and Sargent, 1990; Kleinman, 1980; Lederer, 1995; Ramsey, 1970b; Starr, 1982). Hundreds of experiments of this sort were common practice in the last century, including the forced exposure of military personnel to atomic radiation in the 1940s

A different issue that bioethics embraces pertains to the moral and ethical consequences of technological innovation. For example, a recent newspaper article (Noble, 2000) reported that with the aid of an electronic microchip implanted in his back, a man who had been immobilized for a decade was now able to move his legs. (His spinal cord had been severed in an automobile crash.) The microchip stimulates his leg muscles through electric charges fired by a program in the chip. A spokesperson for the IBM Corporation, which helped develop this technology, reported, "The goal was to give people the possibility of standing and walking. . . . [He] will have to do a great deal of training, and we still face problems in programming the chip with all the intelligence that goes into walking."

On first sight, this appears to be yet another modern marvel of medical and technological innovation. It also serves as a reminder of our increasing dependence on complex technology for our very survival. The first chapter of this book argued that technological and cultural innovations were key in a trajectory that brought us from quadrupedal primates to bipedal bearers of culture. Here it can be observed that earlier in human prehistory, technological innovation assisted our survival. The difference now is that in multiple ways technology controls us.

Technologies also change the ways in which we see and experience the world. North American adults of my parents' generation (born in the 1920s) were raised with the notions that social life was defined by monogamy, that one lived in heterosexual marriage until death, and that divorce resulted in lifelong social ostracism. Recently, I received an e-mail message from a colleague—one that she had sent to scores of others as well. She announced that she and her companion had just "given birth to twins." Two lesbians giving birth to twins? The details of the procedure were not included in the message; nor were the particulars about who was the biological mother and who was the biological father. Emerging technology and the ethics and values that slowly follow behind it thus question in a very fundamental way what seemingly obvious terms such as *mother* and *father* mean. These twin children may never develop a broad understanding of the term *father* and may come to understand the term *mother* to refer to an intrinsically dualistic feminine role. That is what they will see, that is what they will experience, and that is what they will come to think of as the norm. Concurrently, as same-sex marriages become more widely recognized as legal pairings, a growing number of boys and girls will also think of two adult men as normal parents. Either case provides an extreme example of the way in which evolving technology alters the rules of natural phenomena and also highlights the way in which human culture obviates these processes.

THE CULTURE OF NARCISSISM

I rarely watch television, but occasionally I turn on the evening news. Recently my son, who is just about to turn thirteen, was watching with me. Snippets of news stories that run a minute or so are often followed by four or five commercial messages. What is typically advertised is body products, ranging from life insurance for the dead body to products that promise to cure the constipated body, the aching body, the overweight body, the tired body, the aging body, and so on. On this occasion Jason turned to me and said, "Gee, Dad, Americans must *really* be sick!' I think he intended this to mean "unhealthy" or "ailing." But the possibility of double entendre is intriguing.

Perhaps it is better to suggest that contemporary North American culture is awash in body products. Unhappy with our genetically endowed bodies, we are duped into believing that for a price, we can have a fabricated, "ideal" body. As noted at the beginning of this chapter, human beings have most probably been concerned with their bodies, general health, and well-being ever since they attained self-consciousness. Today, however, the body market has inflated to a degree unknown in human history. A large part of this has to do with the ways in which capitalism has turned the body into a commodity and a medium of conspicuous consumption. It is hard to find a strip mall that does not have a fingernail salon; health spas and gyms have multiplied apace; cosmetic surgery is the largest growth specialization in Western medicine. With supermarkets filled with an extraordinary variety and quantity of food, we choose to eat as little as we can as a sign of affluence. In North America there was a time when a stout body served as a sign of success and affluence (as it does in many Asian and African cultures). The current ideal is to appear as though one has just swum the Pacific Ocean, climbed the Andes, and then routed an opponent in a vigorous squash match.

What promotes this vain quest? One answer lies partly in the way that body image is marketed in capitalistic society: "With these products I will have the ideal physical form and will therefore realize astounding success in all I venture." All "happy" people in North America are physically fit. Those who participate in this commerce sense that they are in control of their bodies, when in fact, their behavior is controlled by the mythology of commercialism (see Freedman, 1988; Halperin, 1999; Ogden, 1992;) As Hesse-Biber (1999: 9) observes:

> The single-minded pursuit of thinness and beauty has many parallels to a religious cult. In both cases a group of individuals is committed to a life defined by a rigid set of values and rules. Members of true cults frequently isolate themselves from the rest of the world

and develop a strong sense of community. They seem obsessed with
the path to perfection, which, although unattainable, holds out
compelling promises. In following their ideals, they usually feel
that they are the 'chosen'.

An emerging trend takes this one step further. Rather than travel
to the gym or spa for exercise or physical attention, it is now more fashionable to engage a specialist as one's personal trainer, who will visit at
home. Instead of molding the body in the public sphere of consumption,
the personal trainer provides a service that is private and thus generates greater status and prestige. As depicted in films and the printed
media, all normal people are physical specimens and live in extreme
affluence. Given the fact that most people in North America do not live
in affluence and do not approach this physical ideal, one can only point
to the power of capitalism in successfully promoting a multibillion-dollar industry that is largely based on illusion. As the adage goes, if
advertising didn't work, there wouldn't be any advertising. The fact is,
of course, that advertising does work: we are addicted to an image and
a product few will ever know or own.

As discussed throughout this book, Westerners are not the only
human beings that are incessantly concerned with body image. Sufficient
ethnographic references have been made in order to suggest that this is
a commonality of the human experience: the body bears the costume of
culture. We may be peculiar, however, in the amount of time and money
we devote to the task of making our bodies resemble a cultural ideal.

SOME CLOSING THOUGHTS

Throughout human evolution and known human history, technological innovations have resulted in predicted and unpredictable consequences for their creators. Technological innovations always have social
and cultural consequences. The domestication of fire was cited earlier as
one example of this fact. The domestication of plants and animals had
even wider ramifications. Before writing and documentation emerged in
early city-states, individual persons had considerable autonomy. Writing systems didn't transform the body per se, but they did have a powerful effect on personal freedom and autonomy. In the contemporary
world, electronic technologies can readily transform some of the most
intimate and private parts of our behavior into public knowledge. Most
people have no idea whether or not the FBI or the CIA has their name
on file. Reason suggests that tens of thousands of North American citizens are in fact under the scrutiny of these agencies. The very fact that
we as private citizens do not know about this is ample evidence of one
of the ways in which technology controls both mind and body.

As noted above, emerging technologies, particularly as these relate to medical practice and the human body, have made us ponder anew some basic and primordial human questions. What meaning does life have, or is meaning something we arbitrarily impose upon it? What is human life, and when does it begin? Is brain death really death? Since eggs and sperm can be frozen for indefinite periods of time, should we begin to imagine immortality? Will such questions appear dated in only a short time?

Perhaps human beings will always ask these questions. But as we do, we should also remember that every human being believes that he or she lives in the modern world—the Greeks did, the Romans did, and we do too. Yet as much as we want to believe that technology has made us advanced and modern, our bodies, minds, and emotions retain deep and sometimes volatile fragments of our evolutionary past. Women still tend to select mates as spouses on the belief and assessment that they will be successful providers and protectors for themselves and their potential offspring. In a heartbeat, mothers and fathers will do almost anything to protect their children from danger, or even the threat of danger. On a global scale, thousands of people commit murder on the suspicion of infidelity. Women do not want their husbands to provide material or sexual favors to any but themselves. Men do not want to raise and provide for offspring that they have not sired. Our modernity, in other words, is perpetually clouded by our collective primate history. Scientists now claim that they have mapped the genetic structure of the human being. But thankfully, we are still a long way from mapping human intention, belief, paradox, irony, elation, and remorse, which are collectively frames of mind and emotion that make us what we really are.

The story of our evolutionary success as a species has a single consistent and enduring theme. When technological innovation has not resulted in our immediate death, it has had some greater or lesser role in promoting our lives. In this regard it is not surprising that technological innovations have resulted in moral and ethical dilemmas. It has always been that way. The impact of modern technology on the human body only echoes and recalls some of the most significant moments in our evolutionary history.

In a short book, limited by editorial protocol, it is clearly impossible to address the full range of phenomena that implicate and entail culture and the human body. But when all is said and done, our bodies might be thought of as our only true possession. Still, the matter of how we own them is governed by a system of rules that none of us invented individually, and we live by these rules collectively. To observe the body is to observe culture—not as an abstraction, but in animate form.

Bibliography

Adams, A. E. 1997. "Moulding Women's Bodies." Pp. 59–80 in D. Wilson and C. Laennec (Eds.), *Body Discursions*. Albany: State University of New York Press.

Allyn, D. 1999. *The Sexual Revolution: An Unfettered History*. Boston: Little, Brown.

Andrews, L. 1999, 28 March. "The Sperminator." *New York Sunday Times Magazine*, 62–65.

Annas, G. 1998. *Some Choice: Law, Medicine and the Market*. New York: Oxford University Press.

Anonymous 1968. "What and When Is Death?" *Journal of the American Medical Association* 204: 539–540.

———. 1998, 18 January. "Hair's Vanishing Act." *New York Times*, 38.

Arens, W. 1979. *The Man-Eating Myth: Anthropology and Anthropophagy*. New York: Oxford University Press.

———. 1989. *The Original Sin*. New York: Oxford University Press.

Armelegos, G. 1991. "The Origins of Agriculture: Population Growth during a Period of Declining Health." *Population Environment* 13: 9–22.

Barkan, L. 1975. *Nature's Work of Art: The Human Body as an Image of the World*. New Haven, CT: Yale University Press.

Barker, J., and A. Tietjen. 1990. "Women's Facial Tattooing among the Maisin of New Guinea." *Oceania* 60: 217–234.

Barthes, R. 1983. (Trans. M. Word.). *The Fashion System*. New York: Hill and Wang.

Becker, A. 1995. *Body, Self and Society: The View from Fiji*. Philadelphia: University of Pennsylvania Press.

Beidelman, T. O. 1980. "Women and Men in Two East African Societies." Pp. 143–164 in I. Karp and C. Byrd (Eds.), *Explorations in African Systems of Thought*. Bloomington: Indiana University Press.

———. 1997. *The Cool Knife: Imagery of Gender, Sexuality and Moral Education in Kaguru Initiation Ritual*. Washington, DC: Smithsonian Institution Press.

Bell, C. 1844. *The Anatomy and Philosophy of Expression*. London: George Bell.

Bell, F. 1949. "Tattooing and Scarification on Tonga." *Man* 49: 29–31.

Bell, S. 1994. *Reading, Writing and Rewriting the Prostitute Body*. Bloomington: Indiana University Press.

Benthall, J., and T. Polemus. (Eds.). 1975. *The Body as a Medium of Expression*. London: Pelican.

Berg, C. 1951. *The Unconscious Significance of Hair*. London: George Allen and Unwin.

Bergler, E. 1953. *Fashion and the Unconscious*. New York: Brunner.

Berman, J. 1999. "Bad Hair Days in the Paleolithic: Modern (Re)Constructions of the Cave Man." *American Anthropologist* 101: 288–304.

Berthelot, J. 1986. "Sociological Discourse and the Body." *Theory in Social and Cultural Anthropology* 3: 155–164.

Bettelheim, B. 1968 (1954). *Symbolic Wounds: Puberty Rites and the Envious Male*. New York: Collier Books.

Bickerton, D. 1990. *Language and Species*. Chicago: University of Chicago Press.

Blacking, J. (Ed.) 1977. *The Anthropology of the Body*. New York: Academic Press.

Bloch, M., and J. Parry (Eds.) 1982. *Death and the Regeneration of Life*. Cambridge, MA: Cambridge University Press.

Blumstein, J., and F. Sloan. (Eds.) 1989. *Organ Transplant Policy: Issues and Prospects*. Durham, NC: Duke University Press.

Boddy, J. 1989. *Wombs and Alien Spirits: Women, Men and the Zar Cult in Northern Sudan*. Madison: University of Wisconsin Press.

Bohannan, P. 1956. "Beauty and Scarification amongst the Tiv." *Man* 56: 117–121.

———. 1988 (1965). "The Tiv of Nigeria." Pp. 515–546 in J. Gibbs (Ed.), *Peoples of Africa*. Prospect Heights, IL: Waveland Press.

———. 1988. "Beauty and Scarification Amongst the Tiv." Pp. 77-82 in A. Rubin (Ed.), *Marks of Civilization*. Los Angeles: University of California Museum of Cultural History.

Bouhdiba, A. 1988. *Sexuality in Islam*. London: Routledge and Kegan Paul.

Boyd, J., and J. Silk. 1997. *How Humans Evolved*. New York: W. W. Norton.

Brain, J. 1977. "Sex, Incest and Death: Initiation Rites Reconsidered." *Current Anthropology* 18: 191–208.

———. 1988. "Male Menstruation." *Journal of Psychohistory* 15: 311–323.

Bristow, E. 1983. *Prostitution and Prejudice*. New York: Schocken Books.

Brochdue, V. 1993. *Carved Flesh, Cast Selves: Gendered Symbols and Social Practices*. Oxford: Berg.

Brody, B. 1998. *The Ethics of Biomedical Research*. New York: Oxford University Press.

Brooks, D. 1967. *Resuscitation*. Baltimore, MD: Wilkens and Wilkens.

Brown, D., J. Edwards, and R. Moore. 1988. *The Penis Inserts of Southeast Asia*. Berkeley: Center for South and Southeast Asian Studies.

Brown, J. 1963. "The Cross-Cultural Study of Female Initiation Rites." *American Anthropologist* 65: 837–853.

Bruce, V., and A. Young. 1998. *In the Eye of the Beholder: The Science of Face Perception*. New York: Oxford University Press.

Brundage, J. 1987. *Law, Sex and Christian Society in Medieval Europe*. Chicago: University of Chicago Press.

Bryk, E. 1934. *Circumcision in Man and Woman*. New York: American Ethnological Press.

Bull, R., and N. Rumsey. 1988. *The Social Psychology of Facial Appearance* New York: Springer-Verlag.

Burridge, K. 1979. *Someone, No One: An Essay on Individuality*. Princeton, NJ: Princeton University Press.

Burton, J. W. 1982. "The Names People Play: Atuot Metaphors of Self." *Anthropos* 77: 831–851.

———. 1991. "Representations of the Feminine in Nilotic Cosmology." Pp. 81–98 in A. Jacobson-Widding (Ed.), *Body and Space: Symbolic Modes of Unity and Division in African Cosmology and Experience*. Stockholm: Almqyist and Wiksell.

———. 1999. "Disappearing Savages? Thoughts on the Construction of an Anthropological Conundrum." *Journal of Asian and African Studies* 27: 352–364.

Bynum, C. W. 1971. *Fragmentation and Redemption: Essays on Gender and the Body in Medieval Religion*. New York: Zone Press.

Calebresi, G., and P. Bobbitt. 1978. *Tragic Choices*. New York: Norton.

Camphausen, R. 1997. *Return of the Tribal*. Rochester, VT: Park Street Press.

Caplan, A. 1992. *If I Were a Rich Man, Could I Buy a Pancreas?* Bloomington: Indiana University Press.

Caplan, P. (Ed.). 1980. *The Cultural Construction of Sexuality*. London: Tavistock Publications.

Carmen, A., and H. Moody. 1985. *Working Women: The Subterranean World of Street Prostitution*. New York: Harper and Row.

Carrel, A., and C. Lindburgh. 1938. *The Growth of Organs*. New York: Paul B. Hoeber.

Cheney, D., and R. Seyfarth. 1990. *How Monkeys See the World*. Chicago: University of Chicago Press.

Childe, V. G. 1936. *Man Makes Himself*. London: Watts.

Chomsky, N. 1988. *Language and Problems of Knowledge*. Cambridge, MA: MIT Press.

Clark, J. D., and S. A. Brandt. (Eds.). 1984. *From Hunters to Herders: The Causes and Consequences of Food Production in Africa*. Berkeley: University of California Press.

Cohen, M. N. 1977. *The Food Crisis in Prehistory*. New Haven, CT: Yale University Press.

———. 1989. *Health and the Rise of Civilization*. New Haven, CT: Yale University Press.

Coleridge, N. 1988. *The Fashion Conspiracy*. New York: Harper and Row.

Comaroff, J. 1985. *Bodies of Power, Spirit of Resistance: The Culture and History of a South African People*. Chicago: University of Chicago Press.

Connery, J. 1977. *Abortion: The Development of the Roman Catholic Perspective*. Chicago: Loyola University Press.

Cooper, W. 1971. *Hair: Sex, Society and Symbolism*. New York: Stein and Day.

Corea, G. 1985. *The Mother Machine: Reproductive Technologies from Artificial Insemination to Artificial Wombs*. New York: Harper and Row.

Cummins, D., and C. Allen. (Eds.). 1992. *The Evolution of Mind*. New York: Oxford University Press.

Darwin, C. 1872. *The Expression of Emotions in Man and Animals*. London: John Murray.

Davis, F. 1992. *Fashion, Culture and Identity*. Chicago: University of Chicago Press.

Davis, S. (Ed.). 1988. *Women under Attack*. Boston: South End Press.

Davis-Floyd, R. 1992. *Birth as an American Rite of Passage*. Berkeley: University of California Press.

Davis-Floyd, R., and C. Sargent. (Eds.). 1997. *Childbirth and Authoritative Knowledge*. Berkeley: University of California Press.

Demello, M. 1993. "The Convict Body: Tattooing among Male American Prisoners." *Anthropology Today* 9: 10–13.

De Meo, J. 1997. "The Geography of Male and Female Genital Mutilation." Pp. 1–16 in G. Denniston and M. Milos (Eds.), *Sexual Mutilations*. New York: Plenum Press.

Diamond, J. 1988. "The Arrow of Disease." Pp. 193–199 in E. Angeloni (Ed.), *Anthropology 98/99*. Guilford: Dushkin/McGraw Hill.

———. 1997. *Guns, Germs and Steel: The Fates of Human Societies*. New York: W. W. Norton.

Douglas, M. 1966. *Purity and Danger*. London: Routledge and Kegan Paul.

———. 1970. *Natural Symbols*. London: Barrie and Rockliff.

Douglas, M., and M. Calvez. 1990. "The Self as Risk Taker: A Cultural Theory of Contagion in Relation to AIDS." *Sociological Review* 38: 445–463.

Driver, H. 1969. "Girls Puberty Rites and Matrilocal Residence." *American Anthropologist* 71: 905-908.

Duncan, Y. 1973. "Religious Hair." *Man* 8: 100–103.

Durkheim, E. 1938 (1895). *The Rules of the Sociological Method*. London: Macmillan.

———. 1952 (1897). *Suicide: A Study in Sociology*. London: Routledge and Kegan Paul.

Dworkin, G., and R. Frey. 1998. *Euthanasia and Physician Assisted Suicide*. Cambridge: Cambridge University Press.

East, R. 1965. *Akiga's Story: The Tiv Tribe as Seen by One of Its Members*. London: Oxford University Press.

Ebin, V. 1979. *The Decorated Body*. London: Hudson and Thames.

Evans-Pritchard, E. E. 1956. *Nuer Religion*. Oxford: Clarendon Press.

———. 1960. "Introduction." Pp. 9–24 in R. Hertz, *Death and the Right Hand*. Glencoe, IL: Free Press.

Farazza, A. 1996. *Bodies under Siege*. Baltimore, MD: Johns Hopkins University Press.

Farb, P., and G. Armelegos. 1980. *Consuming Passions: The Anthropology of Eating*. Boston: Houghton Mifflin.

Finkle, J., and A. MacIntosh. (Eds.). 1994. *The New Politics of Reproduction: Conflict and Consensus in Family Planning*. New York: Oxford University Press.

Flaste, R. 1992. *Medicine's Great Journey: One Hundred Years of Healing*. Boston: Little, Brown.

Fletcher, J. 1975. "Abortion, Euthanasia and the Care of the Defective Newborn." *New England Journal of Medicine* 292: 75–79.

Ford, C. S. 1964. *A Comparative Study of Reproduction*. New Haven, CT: Human Relations Area Files.

Fortes, M. 1983. *Rules and the Emergence of Society*. London: Royal Anthropological Institute.

Fox, R. 1967. *Kinship and Marriage*. Harmondsworth, U.K.: Penguin.

———. 1980. *The Red Lamp of Incest*. New York: E. P. Dutton.

Fox, R., and J. Swazey. 1976. *The Courage to Fail: A Social View of Organ Transplants and Dialyses*. Chicago: University of Chicago Press.

Freedman, R. 1988. *Bodylove: Learning to Like Our Looks*. New York: Harper and Row.

Freund, P. (Ed.). 1969. *Ethical Aspects of Experimentation with Human Subjects*. Cambridge, MA: American Academy of Arts and Sciences.

Gaines, J., and C. Herzog. (Eds.). 1990. *Fabrications: Costume and the Human Body*. New York: Routledge and Kegan Paul.

Gaylin, W. 1974. "Harvesting the Dead." *Harpers* 249: 23–30.

Geertz, C. 1973. *The Interpretation of Culture*. New York: Basic Books.

Gell, A. 1993. *Wrapping in Images: Tattooing in Polynesia*. Oxford: Clarendon Press.

Gibson, K., and T. Ingold. (Eds.). 1986. *Tools, Language and Intelligence*. Cambridge: Cambridge University Press.

Giddens, A. 1991. *Modernity and Self-Identity*. Stanford, CA: Stanford University Press.

Gilman, S. 1987. *Disease and Representation: Images of Illness from Madness to AIDS*. Ithaca, NY: Cornell University Press.

Gilmore, D. 1994. "The Beauty of the Beast: Male Body Image in Anthropological Perspective." Pp. 191–214 in M. Winkler and L. Cole (Eds.), *The Good Body: Asceticism in Contemporary Culture*. New Haven, CT: Yale University Press.

Ginsburg, F., and R. Rapp. 1991. "The Politics of Reproduction." *Annual Review of Anthropology* 20: 311–343.

Goffman, E. 1967. *Interaction Ritual: Essays on Face to Face Behavior*. Chicago: Aldine.

Gomez, C. 1991. *Regulating Death*. New York: Free Press.

Grant, M. 1911. *The Passing of the Great Race*. New York: Scribners.

Greenfield, P. 1991. "Language, Tools and the Brain: The Ontology and Phylogeny of Hierarchically Organized Sequential Behavior." *Behavioral and Brain Sciences* 14: 531–595.

Groning, K. 1998. *Body Decoration: A World Survey of Body Art*. New York: Vendome Press.

Gustafson, M. 1997. "*Inscriptia in fronte*: Penal Tattooing in Late Antiquity." *Classical Antiquity* 16: 79–105.

Haiken, H. 1997. *Venus Envy: A History of Cosmetic Surgery*. Baltimore, MD: Johns Hopkins University Press.

Hallpike, C. 1969. "Social Hair." *Man* 4: 256–264.

Halperin, I. 1999. *Shut Up and Smile: Supermodels: The Dark Side*. Los Angeles: Ogo Books.

Handwerker, W. P. (Ed.). 1993. *Births and Power: Social Change and the Politics of Reproduction*. Boulder: Westview Press.

Hartman, B. 1982. *Reproductive Rights and Wrongs*. New York: Harper and Row.

Herdt, G. 1981. *Guardians of the Flutes: Idioms of Masculinity*. New York: McGraw-Hill.

———. (Ed.). 1984. *Ritualized Homosexuality in New Guinea*. Berkeley: University of California Press.

———. 1987. *The Sambia: Ritual and Gender in New Guinea*. New York: Holt, Rinehart and Winston.

Hershman, P. 1974. "Hair, Sex and Dirt." *Man* 9: 275–298.

Hesse-Biber, S. 1999. *Am I Thin Enough Yet? The Cult of Thinness and the Commercialization of Identity*. New York: Oxford University Press.

Hewitt, K. 1997. *Mutilating the Body: Identity in Blood and Ink*. Bowling Green, KY: Bowling Green State University Press.

Hicks, G. 1994. *The Comfort Women: Japan's Brutal Regime of Enforced Prostitution in the Second World War*. New York: W. W. Norton.

Hodges, F. 1997. "A Short History of the Institutionalization of Involuntary Sexual Mutilation." Pp. 17–40 in G. Dennitson and M. Milos (Eds.), *Sexual Mutilations*. New York: Plenum Press.

Hogbin, I. 1996 (1970). *The Island of Menstruating Men*. Prospect Heights, IL: Waveland Press.

Hollander, A. 1980. *Seeing through Clothes*. New York: Aron.

Humphrey, N. 1993. *A History of the Mind*. New York: Harper and Collins.

Hunter, A. n.d. "Body as Battlefield: The Metaphorical Structuring of Borders in Response to Disease." Unpublished manuscript.

Huxley, J. 1941. *Man Stands Alone*. New York: Harpers.

Isaacs, H. 1995. *Idols of the Tribe*. New York: Harper and Row.

Jackson, B. 1997. *Splendid Slippers: A Thousand Years of an Erotic Tradition*. Berkeley: Ten Speed Press.

Johnson, A. 1990. *The New Medicine and the Old Ethics*. Cambridge, MA: Harvard University Press.

Johnson, T., and C. Sargent. (Eds.). 1990. *Medical Anthropology*. New York: Praeger.

Jonsen, A. 1998. *The Birth of Bioethics*. New York: Oxford University Press.

Jonsen, A., and M. Garland. (Eds.). 1992. *Ethics of Newborn Intensive Care*. Berkeley, CA: Institute for Government Studies.

Jordan, B. 1993. *Birth in Four Cultures*, 4th edition. Prospect Heights, IL: Waveland Press.

Joseph, N. 1986. *Uniform and Nonuniforms*. New York: Greenwood Press.

Kaiser, S. 1985. *The Social Psychology of Clothing*. New York: Macmillan.

Kingdon, J. 1993. *Self-Made Man*. New York: John Wiley.

Kitzinger, S., and J. A. Davis. (Eds.). 1978. *The Place of Birth*. New York Oxford University Press.

Kleinman, A. 1980. *Patients and Healers in the Context of Culture*. Berkeley: University of California Press.

Kolata, G. 1997, 23 November. "Clinics Selling Embryos for Adoption: Couples Can Pick Ancestry." *New York Times*, 34.

Korein, J. (Ed.). 1978. *Brain Death*. New York: New York Academy of Sciences.

Laderman, C. 1983. *Wives and Mid-Wives: Childbirth and Nutrition in Rural Malaysia*. Berkeley: University of California Press.

LaFontaine, J. 1985. *Initiation*. Harmondsworth, U.K.: Penguin.

Laitman, J. 1984, August. "The Anatomy of Human Speech." *Natural History*, Pp. 20–27.

Landau, T. 1989. *About Faces*. New York: Doubleday Anchor.

Lang, S. 1998. *Men as Women, Women as Men*. Austin: University of Texas Press.

Langness, L. L. 1999. *Men and 'Women' in New Guinea*. Novato, CA: Chandler & Sharp.

Laquer, T. 1968. *Making Sex: Body and Gender from the Greeks to Freud*. Cambridge, MA: Harvard University Press.

Larsen, C. 1995. "Biological Changes in Human Populations with Agriculture." *Annual Review of Anthropology* 24: 185–213.

Lauer, R., and J. Lauer. 1981. *Fashion Power*. Englewood Cliffs, NJ: Prentice-Hall.

Leach, E. R. 1958. "Magical Hair." *Journal of the Royal Anthropological Institute* 88: 147–164.

———. 1966. "Ritualization in Man in Relation to Conceptual and Social Development." *Philosophical Transactions of the Royal Society*, vol. 251. London: The Royal Society.

Leach, G. 1970. *The Biocrats*. London: Cape.

Leakey, R. 1994. *The Origin of Humankind*. New York: Basic Books.

Lederer, S. 1995. *Subjugated to Science: Human Experimentation in America*. Baltimore, MD: Johns Hopkins University Press.

Leonard, J. 1973. *The First Farmers*. New York: Little, Brown.

Levine, M. 1995. "The Gendered Grammar of Ancient Mediterranean Hair." Pp. 77–130 in H. Eilberg-Schwartz and W. Deniger (Eds.), *Off With Her Head*. Berkeley: University of California Press.

Lévi-Strauss, C. 1966. *Totemism*. Chicago: University of Chicago Press.

———. 1969. *The Elementary Structures of Kinship*. Boston: Beacon Press

———. 1982. *The Way of the Mask*. Vancouver, B. C.: Douglas and McIntyre.

Levy, H. 1966. *Chinese Footbinding: The History of a Curious Erotic Custom*. Tokyo: John Weatherhill.

Liebenberg, L. 1990. *The Art of Tracking*. Cape Town: David Phillip.

Lienhardt, R. G. 1961. *Divinity and Experience: The Religion of the Dinka*. Oxford: Clarendon Press.

———. 1964. *Social Anthropology* London: Oxford University Press

Ligget, J. 1974. *The Human Face*. London: Constable.

Lincoln, B. 1981. *Emerging from the Chrysalis: Studies in Rituals of Women's Initiation*. Cambridge, MA: Harvard University Press.

Linnekin, J., and L. Poyer. 1990. *Cultural Identity and Ethnicity in the Pacific*. Honolulu: University of Hawaii Press.

Livingstone, F. 1958. "Anthropological Implications of Sickle Cell Gene Distribution in West Africa." *American Anthropologist* 60: 533–558.

Lock, M. 1993. "Anthropology and the Epistemologies of Bodily Practice and Knowledge." *Annual Review of Anthropology* 22: 107–132.

Lurie, A. 1981. *The Language of Clothes*. New York: Random House.

Lyon, J. 1985. *Playing God in the Nursery*. New York: Norton.

MacCormack, C. P. (Ed.). 1994. *Ethnography of Fertility and Birth*, 2nd edition. Prospect Heights, IL: Waveland Press.

McCormack, R. 1971. "To Save or Let Die." *Journal of the American Medical Association* 229: 176.

Mageo, J. 1994. "Hairdos and Don't's: Hair Symbolism and Sexual History in Samoa." *Man* 29: 407–423.

Malthus, T. R. 1798. *An Essay on the Principle of Population*. London: J. Johnson.

Mauss, M. 1936. "Les Techniques du Corps." *Journal de Psychologie Normale et Pathologique* 32: 271–293.

Miller, B. 1981. *The Endangered Sex: Neglect of Female Children in Rural North India*. Ithaca, NY: Cornell University Press.

———. 1984.

———. 1987. "Female Infanticide in Rural India." Pp. 44–60 in N. Scheper-Jones (Ed.), *Child Survival: Anthropological Perspectives on the Treatment and Maltreatment of Children*. Boston: Dorrecht.

———. (Ed.). 1993. *Sex and Gender Hierarchies*. Oxford: Oxford University Press.

———. 1997. *The Endangered Sex: Female Children in Rural North India*. Oxford: Oxford University Press.

Miller, L. 1998, 27 October. "Baby Born to Comatose Rape Victim." *New London Day*, 3.

Millet, K. 1971. *The Prostitution Papers*. New York: Ballentine Books.

Miner, H. 1956. "Body Ritual among the Nacirema" *American Anthropologist* 54: 503–507.

Mitford, J. 1992. *The American Way of Death*. New York: Dutton.

Mohr, J. 1978. *Abortion in America: The Origin and Evolution of National Policy, 1800–1900*. New York: Oxford University Press.

Montague, A. 1942. *Man's Most Dangerous Myth: The Fallacy of Race* New York: Columbia University Press.

Moore, F. 1964. *Give and Take: The Development of Tissue Transplantation*. Philadelphia: W. B. Saunders.

Morinis, A. 1985. "The Ritual Experience: Pain and the Transformation of Consciousness in Ordeals of Initiation." *Ethnos*: 13: 150–174.

Morris, D. 1973. *The Naked Ape: A Zoologist's Study of the Human Animal*. New York: Dell.

Napolitan, M. 1939. *Six Thousand Years of Hair Styling*. New York: Polygraphic Company of America.

Needham, R. 1963. Introduction to E. Durkheim and M. Mauss, *Primitive Classification*. Chicago: University of Chicago Press.

———. (Ed.). 1973. *Right and Left: Essays on Dual Symbolic Classification*. Chicago: University of Chicago Press.

———. 1975. "Polythetic Classification: Convergence and Consequences." *Man* 10: 349–369.

———. 1978. *Essential Perplexities* Oxford: Blackwell

———. 1980. *Primordial Characters*. Charlottesville: University Press of Virginia.

Noble, H. 2000, 28 March. "Microchip Helps Paralyzed Man Walk." *New York Times*, D8.

Obeyesekere, O. 1998. "Foreword." Pp. xi–xiv in A. Hitebeitel and B. Miller (Eds.), *Hair: Its Power and Meaning in Asian Cultures*. Albany: State University of New York Press.

Ogden, J. 1992. *Fat Chance: The Myth of Dieting Explained*. London: Routledge.

O'Halon, M. 1989. *Reading the Skin*. London: British Museum.

O'Hara, G. 1986. *The Encyclopedia of Fashion*. New York: Abrams.

Patterson, J. 1987. *The Dread Disease: Cancer and Modern American Culture*. Cambridge: Harvard University Press.

Petchesky, R. 1990. *Abortion and Women's Choice: The State, Sexuality and Reproductive Freedom*. Boston: Northeastern University Press.

Piaget, J. 1932. *The Moral Judgment of the Child*. New York: Free Press.

Piers, M. 1978. *Infanticide*. New York: Norton.

Pinker, S. 1994. *The Language Instinct*. New York: William Morrow.

Plass, P. 1995. *The Game of Death in Ancient Rome: Arena Sport and Political Suicide*. Madison: University of Wisconsin Press.

Polemus, T. (Ed.). 1978. *The Body Reader*. New York: Pantheon Books.

Polemus, T., and L. Proctor. 1978. *Fashion and Antifashion*. London: Thames and Hudson.

Ramet, S. (Ed.). 1996 *Gender Reversals and Gender Culture*. London: Routledge and Kegan Paul.

Ramsey, P. 1970a. *The Patient as Person*. New Haven, CT: Yale University Press.

———. 1970b. *Fabricated Man: The Ethics of Genetic Control*. New Haven, CT: Yale University Press.

———. (Ed.). 1978. *Ethics at the Edges of Life: Medical and Legal Intersections*. New Haven, CT: Yale University Press.

Rapp, R. 1999. *Testing Women, Testing the Fetus: The Social Impact of Amniocentesis in America* . New York: Routledge.

Reiser, S. 1992. "The Intensive Care Unit: The Unfolding Ambiguities of Survival Therapy." *International Journal of Technology Assessment* 8: 382–394.

Rigby, P. 1967. "The Structural Context of Girls' Puberty Rites." *Man* 2: 343–444.

Rorrik, D. 1978. *In Ilis Image: The Cloning of Man*. New York: Henry Holt.

Rosaldo, M., and L. Lamphere. (Eds.). 1974. *Women, Culture and Society*. Stanford, CA: Stanford University Press.

Rosenblatt, D. 1997. "The Antisocial Skin: Structure, Resistance and 'Modern Primitive' Adornment in the U.S." *Cultural Anthropology* 12: 287–334.

Rothman, B. 1982. *In Labor: Women and Power in the Birthplace*. New York: W. W. Norton.

Rubin, A. (Ed.). 1988. *Marks of Civilization*. Los Angeles: Museum of Cultural History.

Rudofsky, B. 1971. *The Unfashionable Body*. New York: Doubleday.

Sainders, D., and M. Baines. 1983. *Living with Dying: The Management of Terminal Disease*. New York: Oxford University Press.

Sanders, C. 1988. "Drill and Frill: Client Choice, Client Typologies and Interactional Control in Commercial Tattooing." Pp. 219–231 in B. Rubin (Ed.), *Marks of Civilization*. Los Angeles: Museum of Cultural History.

———. 1989. *Customizing the Human Body*. Philadelphia: Temple University Press.

Sargent, C. 1989. *Maternity, Medicine and Power: Reproductive Decisions in Urban Benin*. Berkeley: University of California Press.

Scarry, E. 1985. *The Body in Pain*. New York: Oxford University Press.

Schilder, P. 1950. *The Image and Appearance of the Body*. New York: International Universities Press.

Schragger, D. n.d. "The Concept of the Human Body as Property." Unpublished manuscript.

Schwartz, T. 1973. "Cult and Context: The Paranoid Ethos in Melancsia." *Ethnos* 1: 153–174.

Scott, R. 1981. *The Body as Property*. New York: Viking Press.

Sheets-Johnstone, M. 1990. *The Roots of Thinking*. Philadelphia: Temple University Press.

Shilling, C. 1993. *The Body and Social Theory*. London: Sage.

Siebald, C. 1992. *The Hospice Movement: Easing Death's Pain*. New York: McMillan International.

Slack, P. 1988. "Response to Plague in Early Europe." *Social Research* 55: 433–451.

Sontag, S. 1989. *AIDS and Its Metaphors*. New York: Farrar, Strauss and Girou.

Starr, P. 1982. *The Social Transformation of American Medicine*. New York: Basic Books.

Stead, D. 1999, 2 March. "Circumcision's Pain and Benefits Re-examined." *New York Times*, D6.

Steiner, C. 1990. "Body Personal and Body Public: Adornment and Leadership in Cross-Cultural Perspective." *Anthropos* 85: 431–445.

Steiner, F. 1999. *Selected Writings*. New York: Berghahn Books.

Stoddard, L. 1920. *The Rising Tide of Color against White Supremacy*. Westport, CT: Negro University Press.

Strong, C. 1997. *Ethics in Reproduction and Perinatal Care*. New Haven, CT: Yale University Press.

Sydie, R. 1987. *Natural Woman, Cultural Man*. New York: New York University Press.

Synott, A. 1993. *The Body Social: Symbolism, Self and Society*. London: Routledge and Kegan Paul.

Tannahill, R. 1988. *Food in History*. New York: Crown Publishers.

Tannenbaum, N. 1987. "Tattoos: Invulnerability and Power in Shan Cosmology." *American Ethnologist* 14: 693–710.

Thevoz, M. 1984. *The Painted Body*. New York: Rizzoli.

Tiemersma, D. 1989. *Body Schema and Body* Image Amsterdam: Swets and Zeitlinger.

Tiger, L. 2000, 18 March. *New York Sunday Times Book Review*, p. 30.

Titmus, R. 1971. *The Gift Relationship: From Human Blood to Social Policy*. London: George Allen and Unwin.

Turner, B. S. 1984. *The Body and Society: Explorations in Social Theory*. Oxford: Blackwell.

Turner, T. 1980. "The Social Skin." Pp. 112–140 in J. Cherfas and R. Lewin (Eds.), *Not Work Alone: A Cross-Cultural View of Activities Superfluous to Survival*. Beverly Hills, CA: Sage.

Turner, V. 1969. *The Ritual Process*. Chicago: Aldine.

United States Government. 1981. *Defining Death: A Report on the Medical, Legal and Ethical Issues on the Determination of Death*. Washington, DC: Government Printing Office.

Van Gennep, A. 1960 (1909). (Trans. M. Vizedom and G. Caffee.) *The Rites of Passage*. Chicago: University of Chicago Press.

Veatch, R. 1976. *Death, Dying and the Biological Revolution*. New Haven, CT: Yale University Press.

Walker, A., and P. Parmar. 1993. *Warrior Marks: Female Genitle Mutilation and the Sexual Binding of Women*. New York: Harcourt Brace.

Walters, L., and J. Palmer. 1976. *The Ethics of Human Gene Therapy*. New York: Oxford University Press.

Warnock, M. 1985. *A Question of Life*. Oxford: Blackwell.

Waywell, B. n.d. "Technology Facts." Unpublished manuscript.

Weiner, A., and J. Schneider. (Eds.). 1989. *Cloth and Human Experience*. Washington, DC: Smithsonian Institution Press.

Weisberg, D. 1985. *Children of the Night*. Lexington: D.C. Heath.

West, D. 1993. *Male Prostitution*. New York: The Harwood Press.

Wheeler, P. P. 1984. "The Evolution of Bipediality and the Loss of Functional Body Hair in Humans." *Journal of Human Evolution* 13: 91–98.

Whiteford, L., and M. Poland. (Eds.). 1989. *New Approaches to Human Reproduction*. Boulder, CO: Westview Press.

Wills, C. 1993. *The Runaway Brain*. New York: Basic Books.

Wilson, D. S., and C. M. Laennec. (Eds.). 1997. *Body Discursions*. Albany: State University of New York Press.

Winslow, D. 1980. "Rituals of First Menstruation in Sri Lanka." *Man* 15: 603–625.

Wolfe, A. 1993. *The Human Difference*. Berkeley: University of California Press.

Young, F. 1965. *Initiation Ceremonies: A Cross Cultural Study of Status Differentiation*. New York: Bobbs-Merrill.

Index

122   Index

Birth. *See* Birthing culture; Childbirth
Birth as an American Rite of Passage
    (Davis-Floyd), 38
Birthing culture, in mass and face-to-
    face societies, 38–40
Birthing technology, 92, 95
Blood transfusion, 96
Boas, Franz, 25
Boddy, Janice, 43–44
Body. *See* Human body
Body control, 32–44. *See also* Human
    body
Body Decoration (Groning), 3
Body hair, 46–47. *See also* Hair
    removal techniques, 47
Body image, 3–4
Body painting, 60. *See also* Tattooing
Body products, 105–106
Body transformation. *See* Cosmetic
    surgery; Piercing; Scarification;
    Tattooing
Bohannan, Laura and Paul, 82–83
Boot camp, 34
Boyd, J., 9
Boys. *See* Adolescents; Childbirth;
    Children; Males; Men; Puberty
Brahmins, 34
Braidwood, Robert, 19–20
Brain
    complexity of, 11
    hair and, 14
    language and, 16–17
Brain, J., 72
Brown, J., 72
Bruce, V., 57
Bumi people, 60
Burial. *See also* Death and dying;
    Funeral rites
    secondary, 49
Burridge, K., 31

Calls, as communication, 16
Care at the End of Life Campaign,
    103
Castes, in India, 33–34
Castration, male circumcision and, 72
Childbirth, 35–38
    birthing culture and, 38–40
    among Sambian people, 74

Childe, V. Gordon, 19
Children. *See also* Childbirth
    culture, biology, and, 35–36
    naming of, 55
    play of, 28
Chimpanzees, dyadic grooming by, 14
China, foot binding in, 62–63
Chomsky, Noam, 16
Christian Scientists, 61
Circumcision
    female, 41–44
    among Kaguru peoples, 79–80
    male, 42
    in military, 34–35
    ritual, 34, 71
    among Tiv people, 82, 84
    views of, 72–73
Class endogamy, 57
Clitoridectomy, 42–44
    role of ritual in, 71
Clothing, 66–68
Collective, individual and, 29–31
Common sense rules, 27
Communication. *See also* Language
    body for, 2
    human language and, 16
    verbal, 11
Conception, fashions of, 94–96
Conscious/unconscious experiences,
    29
Contraceptives, 92
Cooking, 13. *See also* Food
Cooling, 14
Cooper, W., 46
Corporate culture, body control in, 35
Cortés, Hernando, 21–22, 58
Cosmetic surgery, 59, 61–63
Cosmologies, 32
Couvade, 36
Cranial capacity, 11, 12
Cranial deformation, 62
Cremation, 49
Crowd diseases, 21–22
Culture. *See also* Language; specific
    issues
    ethnicity and, 53
    fire and, 13–14
    interaction and, 25
    invention of, 8–9